The twits

Real Celebrities. Real Tweets. Real Funny.

Quinn Conroy

sourcebooks

Published by Sourcebooks, Inc.
P.O. Box 4410, Naperville, Illinois 60567-4410
(630) 961-3900
Fax: (630) 961-2168
www.sourcebooks.com

Printed and bound in the United States of America.
VP 10 9 8 7 6 5 4 3 2 1

#Contents

#Introduction

It seems like every day there's another celebrity or politician in trouble for something they said on Twitter. Apparently, no matter how much fame or money you have, there's still something appealing to sharing your thoughts 140 characters at a time. For some, it's a way to stroke their substantial egos. For others, it seems to be a way to share their unlimited supply of comedic gold. Good or bad, celebrities who tweet give us a peek into their lives like never before.

On the following pages, you'll find feuds galore—from Demi Moore versus Kim Kardashian, to Lindsay Lohan versus…well, just about everyone. You'll see that big heads like Kanye West and The Situation are obvious, even in their tweets.

But let's not forget the ultimate kind of celebrity twit—the crazypants one! Lucky for us, celebrity tweets provide just about as much straight-up nonsense as we can possibly handle. (I'm looking at you, Charlie Sheen.)

Sometimes they're sharing bizarre parts of their lives, like pop star Ke$ha live-tweeting the process of peeing her pants.

Beyond the stupid and ridiculous, there are genuinely funny celebrities, like Stephen Colbert and Roger Ebert, who especially excel at cramming their personal brand of humor into 140 characters. We've left all the tweets as-is, misspellings and all, unless otherwise noted. It all makes for an unprecedented look at the Twits—those tweeting celebrities with something to say.

#LifeLessons

Celebrities are always willing to share their knowledge, even when they're total idiots. Here are some of the best life lessons celebrities have to offer.

ITS FRIDAY NIGHT! Remember- Don't drink the pee-pee!

—*Diddy*

The more you learn the less you know.

—*Gary Busey*

Fur pillows are hard to actually sleep on

—*Kanye West*

If you are gonna jump rope, don't forget a bra. I've been hittin' myself in the face all morning.

—*Holly Madison*

why did i take my shirt off for the cover of rolling stone? that will haunt me to my grave. thats official douchebag behavior.
—*Pete Wentz*

Sexting leads to trouble but painting messages on each other's bodies with washable paints or markers can only lead to fun…and sex!
—*Dr. Ruth*

side boob just changed my life
—*Ke$ha*

A fart in a glass is still a fart!
—*Boy George*

I'm not saying don't eat at a place that has pictures of the food on their menu, I'm just saying wear a diaper when you do.
—*Rob Delaney*

If you're over 18 or under 60, let's take a real hard look at the pomp and circumstance surrounding your birthday party.

—*Mindy Kaling*

I have business meetings all day. Ran out of house. On way to first one and just realized I forgot a bra! Ya kidding me?

—*Tori Spelling*

Please don't mistake my weakness for kindness, wait can u flip that?

—*Jeremy Piven*

A woman has to have her Feet looking right in my opinion!

—*Nick Cannon*

In 50 years, a bunch of 80 year-olds will know all the words to The Fresh Prince of Bel-Air theme song.

—*Jonah Hill*

4 students: do ur homework on Fridays cuz then won't be haunting u all weekend. i used 2 do it soon as I got hme. fri, sat, sun was fun then!

—*Tyra Banks*

THIS IS A PSA: NOBODY SHOULD EAT 7/11 NACHOS AT 3am AND GO RIGHT TO SLEEP OR YOU SHALL FEEL THE RATH OF THE CORNER STORE GODS N THE MORNING!

—*T-Pain*

Went to a trendy gay beach in Mykonos called Elia. Lots of posturing, lots of exposed aged wieners. It was all rather intimidating.

—*Neil Patrick Harris*

By the way, everyone sounds like CRAIG FERGUSON in GLASGOW!!!!

—*Jackie Collins*

P.S. I'm not a tv show lol

—*Lindsay Lohan*

You basically can say anything to someone on an email or text as long as you put LOL at the end

—*Kanye West*

love is like my dick. it gets hard.

—*Soulja Boy*

It occurred to me that sometimes even I have no idea what I'm talking about. I just like the sound of my words. Who cares what they mean?

—*Stan Lee*

Guys! A sure-fire way to let a gal know you like her is to press your boner into the small of her back while she's sleeping! Give it a try!

—*Andy Richter*

Attention men in public restrooms: when pooping, you don't have to make mouth noises.

—*Rainn Wilson*

Yoko Says:

Imagine a dolphin dancing in the sky. Let it dance with joy. Think of yourself at the bottom of the ocean watching.

—*Yoko Ono*

#Ke$haLiveTweetsPeeing HerPants

Ke$ha, the pop star known for first bringing the world poetic lyrics like, "When I leave, brush my teeth with a bottle of Jack," found herself in need of a bathroom while on the road—and decided to share.

I'm gonna pee my pants.

—Ke$ha

I can't pull over.

—Ke$ha

There are no big gulps in the car

—Ke$ha

I'm at a loss.

—Ke$ha

Kageling like a mofo

—Ke$ha

#WilliamShatner

William Shatner's tweets are a mixture of Dad jokes and beat poetry. But nothing beats a special guest appearance by fellow *Star Trek* veteran Leonard Nimoy, who, of course, ends each of his tweets with "LLAP" (Live Long and Prosper).

#youknowyoureoldwhen Your warm-up becomes your workout. My best, Bill
—*William Shatner*

Keeping and eye out for speed traps. One eye on the hoagie, one eye on the speed traps. **#whatdoyouthink**
—*William Shatner*

Someone just asked me if I know who owns the legal rights to my face. Either way, you couldn't afford it. My best, Bill
—*William Shatner*

#youknowyoureoldwhen little old ladies help you across the street. My best, Bill
—*William Shatner*

Me riding a horse is the purest form of entertainment I know. My best, Bill
—*William Shatner*

I've been told my damaged star on the Canadian Walk of Fame has been fixed. I wish I could replace my face as easily. My best, Bill
—*William Shatner*

Don't get in a 1500lb pumpkin. When you emerge you'll be out of your gourd. My best, Bill
—*William Shatner*

@williamshatner Bill: Just saw promo for your new show. Glad you finally have something useful to do with your life. LLAP

—*Leonard Nimoy*

@TheRealNimoy Lenny, it's your time to pay for a meal. I must talk to you about how you're wasting your life. My best, Bill

—*William Shatner*

@williamshatner. You're working, you pay!! Did you forget your wallet? LLAP

—*Leonard Nimoy*

Yoko Says:

Let's report to the Universe how glad we are that our planet is part of a beautiful constellation.

—*Yoko Ono*

#NameDropping

The random gossip, interactions, and schmoozing in Hollywood can make for some surprises. Who knew Courtney Love and Whitney Houston once ate turkey chili in a bedroom together?

Time to get my shit together today…
gonna make a statue of **@JohnStamos**
with it.

—Bob Saget

Will Ferrell keeps driving past my house in a tiny French car, laughing and waving a razor. He is a cruel man with lots of free time.

—Conan O'Brien

Dear ashton Kutcher yo mamma so old the key on ben franklins kite, was to her apartment. Respond if yur not scared

—Shaquille O'Neal

I hope this doesn't break any of those patient/doctor confidentiality laws, but it is true: **@ladygaga** & I share the same gynecologist.

—Joy Behar

My water just broke.

—Lady Gaga

Yall aint gone believe this shit I just got off a plane. The flight attendant told me puffy don't flush the toilet

—50 Cent

It is just plain not humanly possible to dislike Taylor Swift.

—Roger Ebert

On my way to tape Late Night With **@JimmyFallon**. If you don't hear from me within 24 hours, you know where to look

—Keith Olbermann

@**chriscrocker** my opinion of Whitney Houston? IMagine this, it really happened, me and her in my bedroom eating Turkey Chili, it was like snl skit

—Courtney Love

Russell Brand is beyond funny. I cannot keep a straight face working with him.

—Alec Baldwin

I have decided to be @**Alec_Baldwin**'s angriest twitter follower.

—Steve Martin

So excited! I'm off to have dinner tonight with Judge Judy! Do you think it's rude if I bring some of my parking tickets for her to "fix"?

—Joan Rivers

Just realized **@kanyewest** follows 0 so had to unfollow him for the safety of his spiritual well being!

—*Boy George*

It's tough sharing a birthday with Kourtney Kardashian. Our friends never know which party to go to.

—*Conan O'Brien*

Shook Sharon Stone's hand last night. SS 2 me: "Nice to see you, Congratulations." Imma start sayin' congrats 2 everyone I meet now.

—*Elizabeth Banks*

I have no idea what SS was congratulating me for but I like to think it was just for making it to that moment in time.

—*Elizabeth Banks*

Saw Chris Rock last night. He said, "Hey, Chelsea Handler!" We've met before. I'm 98.65% positive he was not kidding. I didn't correct him.

—Elizabeth Banks

Steve Carell is kinda sexy

—Ke$ha

@**[Larry King]** Hi Larry Queen! xx!

—Boy George

@**drdrew** Worried bout u, dude…Dr. Dude.

—Eric Roberts

Took William H Macy and my boys on a great Sunday Harley ride to Ojai today. Had lunch w Bill Paxton. Good times.

—Fred Durst

Tonight really messed up my bathroom habits. Now I have this weird thing where I can't go unless Letterman is around.

—*Stephen Colbert*

met **@ladygaga** n went 2 her concert. TALENTED 4 REALZ! N a damn good person!!! After spndng time/ her, Gaga now high on my list of good chix!

—*Tyra Banks*

Sat next to 50 Cent on the plane. Great guy. Had that awkward "when do we put on the iPod headphones and end the convo moment" about 4 times

—*Jonah Hill*

forgot to mention i was face to face with harrison ford at whole foods yesterday he seemed frantic like he was still in the "fugitive"

—*Sandra Bernhard*

Lance Armstrong is the only guy in the world who can tweet while getting a massage and be cool.

—*Ben Stiller*

The true power in the Kardashians is their ability to make hideously unsexy things like diet pills, adult diapers and toilet paper, sexy.

—*Mindy Kaling*

Stephen Colbert STOLE my mother f-ing Grammy!

—*Kathy Griffin*

Patton Oswalt and I are sitting in the audience, texting each other like a couple of 12-year-old girls

—*Al Yankovic*

Hope when I turn 60 I can think, quietly, "My wife is being born somewhere." **#hefner**

—*Patton Oswalt*

Dinner at Sunset Tower. Spotted Jon Hamm of MAD MEN. Soooo handsome, beard & all
—*Jackie Collins*

Is that Yoko Ono across the room? I can't tell. I'll do fake trip 2the bathroom to get a closer look at her. Maybe will drop a pen at her table
—*Tyra Banks*

Busy last two days. Did "A Very Stupid Conversation" in Chicago with Martin Short. Very fun and audience seemed to like me best.
—*Steve Martin*

I love my friend Lance Bass!
—*Debbie Gibson*

Just landed in NYC and got a nice scary surprise from Teri Hatcher! She came up behind me and scared me so bad I screamed! Love u Teri! Xo

—Kim Kardashian

@**EvaLongoria** Thanks so much Eva for graciously welcoming me into Twitter world. Work was fun this morning. My boob is still tingling. Ha!

—Teri Hatcher

I <3 Enrique Iglesias

—Lindsay Lohan

Ke$ha texted me.

—Andrew WK

Listening to R. Kelly – Mister sex on two legs.

—Jackie Collins

#MichaelIanBlack

Twitter's given some comics an outlet to the evil voices in their heads at any given moment. Michael Ian Black, actor on *The State*, *Ed*, and *Reno 911!*, likes to walk the fine line between funny and completely offensive.

Idea for if I ever have to execute one of Santa's elves: Christmas light noose.

—*Michael Ian Black*

Wife was offended when I said she smelled "yeasty."

—*Michael Ian Black*

My wife is watching Madonna videos with my daughter; I have naked pictures of all three.

—*Michael Ian Black*

If I was a baseball player I would ask for pants that don't make me look I'm wearing an extra ass on my ass.

—*Michael Ian Black*

Salt Lake City is the biggest, cleanest white supremacist compound I've ever seen.

—*Michael Ian Black*

Starting to think no matter who is the next president, I will still have allergies. Politics are such bullshit.

—*Michael Ian Black*

IMPORTANT!!! IMPORTANT!!! IMPORTANT!!! MINI WHEATS ARE DELICIOUS!!!

—*Michael Ian Black*

If I've said it once I've said it a thousand times: "it." HA HA HA HA HA! I'M AN AMAZING COMEDIAN!!!

—*Michael Ian Black*

Instead of "handicapped," I prefer the term "handincapableofwalking."

—*Michael Ian Black*

Yoko Says:

Imagine 1000 suns in the sky @ same time. Let them shine for 1hr. Then let them gradually melt into the sky. Make 1 tunafish sandwich & eat.

—*Yoko Ono*

#Ice-T

Ice-T is gangster turned rapper turned *Law and Order: SVU* TV cop turned obsessive tweeter turned reality show star. He has a "Twitter gang" called Final Level Twitter Gang. No, seriously. He's married to a model named Coco, who tweets pictures of herself in a thong every Thursday. You can't make this up.

You think you've seen people dance? You've never seen anyone dance till you hear Maury Povich say…"You are NOT the father!"

—*Ice-T*

To all the guys that follow my wife…And diss me…I totally understand.

—*Ice-T*

Bill O'Reilly is a racist bitch… Point blank. Fuck him and who ever is down with him.

—*Ice-T*

I'm at a photo shoot with @[**Coco**] and ALL the girls are squeezing her booty…All I hear is "incredible…It is real!" Wow. Women trip.

—*Ice-T*

It's funny how MFs get their feelings hurt when I BLOCK em…BUT I warned them… Don't diss or test me on my fuckin page! That = BLOCKED

—*Ice-T*

This may sound strange… But I don't trust people that don't like dogs…

—*Ice-T*

Yoko Says:

This is an invisible tree safe from somebody trying to cut down.

—*Yoko Ono*

#CelebritiesAreObsessedWith FartsAndPoop

Celebrities love tweeting about their gas and crap. Celebrities: They're just like that annoying friend on Facebook who overshares! Except, well…they're rich.

I just farted, sources close to me can confirm.

—*John Mayer*

I took a prenatal vitamin by mistake this morning so my next few farts will probably be able to do simple math.

—*Rob Delaney*

Somene who laughs so hard they poo their pants. LOL

—*Ricky Martin*

WHY, no matter how old I get, are farts so f@!king funny!?!

—*Nicole Richie*

@petewentz describe in detail what your farts smell like

—*Nicole Richie*

@nicolerichie flowers and unicorns. unless i eat mcdonalds and then they just smell like big macs.

—*Pete Wentz*

Shitting your pants definitely takes you down a couple suave notches.

—*Sarah Silverman*

I was awakened in the middle of the night by the sound of my own fart.

—*Rivers Cuomo*

Little hong kong businessman on AA flt#250 sitting in 5E I know its YOU who is tooting like apck mule. The whole cabin is in agony!

—*Billy Bush*

in boston trying to pee but not poo in bus which is quite a skill unto itself

—*Margaret Cho*

Your hole is all "what about me? What about my needs?"

—*Margaret Cho*

I don't wanna be THAT guy, but I'm pretty sure one of these strippers had a butt burp -_-

—*T-Pain*

I just farted 10 times… Once on every step as I was walking… Just thought I'd share that with FLTG.

—Ice-T

I remember when I used to have to fart in my car on a date… I would stop, get out and act like something was wrong with the tire & fart.

—Ice-T

Since I'm on one… You haven't had a REAL Orgasam until you've cum-yelled-farted & got a headache at the same time. 'The Final Level'

—Ice-T

Ladies… If you can make your mad do that! You're a keeper… Now you all know Coco's secret. 4 way explosions! NearDeathExperience

—Ice-T

Back to farts: I honestly have never smelled one of Coco's farts but she can tell the difference between mine & our dogs. I try to blame him

—Ice-T

Just had a quiet lunch end with the waitress accidentally letting out a super loud FART. The odor drove us away. I felt so bad for her. :-(

—Fred Durst

My doctor jus told me that wen you have gas, to never feel alone because in a room, just abt everybody is holding a fart. HAHAHAHA!!!!

—Macy Gray

I've gotta go take a dump right now. BRB!
—Perez Hilton

Not sure I should share this, but I used this port-a-potty and now see there's no toilet paper. Using $1 bills instead.

—Andrew WK

Signs are everywhere. I just tooka shit that was in the shape of an arrow. I'm gonna follow it.

—Dane Cook

Yoko Says:

Make a promise to a tree. Ask it to be passed on to other trees.

—Yoko Ono

#BritneySpears

Britney Spears usually has her handlers tweet boring publicity blasts for her. Except for one glorious day, when she shared all three of the thoughts she had been storing in her head for so long. Snooki approved.

Does anyone think global warming is a good thing? I love Lady Gaga. I think she's a really interesting artist.

—*Britney Spears*

Yes. I love to act and would love to be in a Todd Philips or Judd Apatow movie.

—*Britney Spears*

@britneyspears God how I've missed you. Love your soul.

—*Snooki*

#DeepThoughtsWithLarryKing

Larry King has a lot of profound questions and concerns about the world, dammit! Won't someone give him the answers he needs?

Why do people say something is "as cute as a button"? Why not as cute as a zipper?
—*Larry King*

Did they ever determine, "Who let the Dogs Out?"
—*Larry King*

What ever happened to station wagons?
—*Larry King*

When Twitter is over capacity and there are "too many tweets"…why is there a picture of birds carrying a whale? What does that mean!?
—*Larry King*

Why does Starbucks call a small coffee "tall"? Have you seen those cups? There's really nothing tall about them…

—*Larry King*

I just fed my dog and on the dog food bag it says "DELICIOUS!" How do they know?

—*Larry King*

Why is the #2 pencil so popular? Why is #2 treated like #1?

—*Larry King*

What are you supposed to say when God sneezes?

—*Larry King*

Was about to Tweet, "No one has ever improved on yellow mustard" and realized I'm turning into Larry King

—*Patton Oswalt*

#ADayInTheLife

Celebrities' daily lives are just like ours! Surely you've had a recent altercation with a stripper or spent $3,000 on pillows, only to get scolded by your rock star spouse? No? OK, well, never mind then. They're nothing like us.

Was awoken this morning to my daughter telling me that I had no shot at ever winning the Nobel Peace Prize.

—Ben Stiller

Tweet from my horse- no joke. a first anywhere?

—Michael Keaton

A stripper tryed to kill me this week end

—Danny Bonaduce

I really think my dog Dingo is a vampire!! He will not walk into my house until I invite him!!

—Lance Bass

i slept with glass in my mouth

—*Courtney Love*

Every time a DC # comes up on my phone I instinctually think it's my father's press secretary and I've done something requiring "discussion"

—*Meghan McCain*

Just spent a good 1/2 hr. imagining gracefully forgiving people who were apologizing for wronging me over the years.

—*Rob Delaney*

An episode of the jersey shore just happened at I HOP. Some roid boy just tried to start a fight with me. I had to hold my husband back.

—*Pink*

On the plane and wondering why my pillowcase has chocolate on it.

—*Kristin Chenoweth*

Do you ever look at your credit card bill & ask your wife how the hell she could spend 3 thousand dollars on pillows? I do. PILLOWS.

—*Joel Madden*

That's why i ignore your calls RT **@JoelMadden**: Do you ever look at your credit card bill & ask your wife how the hell she could spend 3 thousand dollars on pillows?

—*Nicole Richie*

Needless to say the pillows are going back to the expensive ass pillow store. I hope she likes the Target pillows I'm putting in their place

—*Joel Madden*

insomnia time = draw wieners on
@JoelMadden's face time.

—Nicole Richie

I think I might wear my MC Hammer
trousers today. They enable me to move
sideways at alarming speeds and provide
commodious ball comfort.

—Simon Pegg

Preparing for Ellen show with lipo and
nosejob. Tapes at 3:30pm. Heal! Heal!

—Steve Martin

I went to lunch at the Plaza. I asked the
piano player to play a song from Phantom
of the Opera and then asked a good
looking guy to dance.

—Dr. Ruth

Jeez! Gardeners in my hood are going crazy. Leaves round here get blown more than Mick Jagger.

—*Craig Ferguson*

@ work screaming CHI TOWN!!!!!!!!!!!!!!!!!!!!!!
—*Jeremy Piven*

1st day was ok, rough start. Very interesting location. Not easy teaching civilians how to be REAL law enforcement.

—*Steven Seagal*

Wardrobe, Wardrobe, Wardrobe
—*Steven Seagal*

Whenever I pass kids who are sitting in 1st class as I board a plane, I ask them if they heard that Santa Claus was murdered.

—*Rob Delaney*

I just went to pee pee and my bathroom's so big I almost peed in the sauna.

—*Pink*

My 3rd year old is upstairs stomping around screaming, "Where's my knife?! Where's my knife?!" So Proud. **#raisingaDanielDayLewisCharacter**

—*Joel McHale*

Just now hairstylist (who shall remain nameless) abused me w/a curling iron whil trying to curl and dancing to my new song…ow

—*Mariah Carey*

I'm searching for some aloe or whatever but its not looking pretty…its basically a welt… Oh the trials and tribulations Divadom!

—*Mariah Carey*

Now he's all trying to put toothpaste on it and swears its a home remedy, I'm like "Stop crying, you're NOT fired" lol

—*Mariah Carey*

For $15 I'll induce your labor

—*Tracy Morgan*

For every hair I lose from my head, I receive a compensatory hair in my ear or nose. Elsewhere Mother Nature pisses her leafy knickers.

—*Simon Pegg*

I'm a mother, actress, comedienne & talk show host yet I'm wigless, homeless & sitting on the stairs waiting for a locksmith cuz I lost keys

—*Sherri Shepherd*

I can't believe my grand mothers making me take Out the garbage I'm rich fuck this I'm going home I don't need this shit

—*50 Cent*

I've got an under the skin zit on my nose that is invisible but I can feel. It's like I have a guilty secret. Which I do. My love of ham.

—*Craig Ferguson*

I'd wear any of my private attire for the world to see. But I would rather have an open flesh wound than ever wear a band aid in public.

—*Lady Gaga*

#whythesouthfuckingrules nascar shirts at goodwill. Lots of em.

—*Ke$ha*

Just had my den redone. Really turned on cause the carpet matches the drapes.

—*Bob Saget*

Im buying another phantom. Trading in my lambo and Bentley and im getting a driver. Im tired of looking at the cops 2 times out the week gnr

—*Bow Wow*

I'm out gucci bike shopping. What color do my babies think I should get?

—*Lil' Kim*

I didn't tweet yesterday because I've focused on xmas shopping on the internet. My thumb hurts from clicking the buttons. Holidays R stressful

—*Coco*

Sleet and gale warnings have postponed my pheasant hunt. Never imagined saying any of those words.

—*Melissa Joan Hart*

I just sprayed myself with bubblegum perfume! I wanna chew myself so badly right now!!!

—*Tyra Banks*

Mum, today is Groundhog Day. I will spend all day watching Groundhog Day; which is what I did yesterday. Send condoms.

—*Russell Brand*

I thought I saw myself on TV, turns out it was Bill Murray in What About Bob

—*Nicole Richie*

This weekend I'm going to try to find out if I'm connected to the moon.

—*David Lynch*

I'm pretty sure I'm connected to the moon.

—*David Lynch*

Katy Perry's vagina is trending!!!!
AMAZING!!!!!!!!!!!!

—*Perez Hilton*

sorry mom.

—*Katy Perry*

Just heard a homeless man say 'you have to be pro-active with your time management' to his drunk friend. only in nyc do we have yuppie bums.

—*Moby*

If someone in this CVS is following me on Twitter, please open up another register. My Flavor Ice Pops are melting.

—*Conan O'Brien*

It occurred to me this morning, as I was pumping my milk whilst reading Twitter, my life would seem odd to the Amish.

—*Alyson Hannigan*

Yoko Says:

Imagine tying balloons to the roof of every building in the city. Let the balloons wave to the breeze. See if the buildings are lighter for it.

—*Yoko Ono*

#50CentAndOprahTheDog

When you hear the name 50 Cent, you might think of a gangster turned rapper who came out with a really crappy movie a while back. You might not know that A) he has a miniature schnauzer named Oprah with a tiny pink cast on its leg or that B) he pretended to have broken the dog's leg to mess with PETA supporters or that C) he set up a Twitter account for Oprah the Dog and tweeted from it.

So now I guess I have beef with the peta people damn everybody hates chris I mean curtis. lol

—50 Cent

This is my dog Oprah Winfrey. I broke her leg cause the peta people threw paint on my coat. Fuck that! [photo with Oprah]

—50 cent

50 is crazy I want a new fuckin owner he broke my leg goddamn it!

—Oprah the Dog

motherfucker 50 almost stepped on me this morning and he knew I was at the foot of the bed. and he always calling me for nothing!!

—Oprah the Dog

and he always plays his music too loud. dont nobody wanna hear that shit! he aint made a classic since get rich or die tryin

—Oprah the Dog

he expects me to jump through hoops for a treat! sit…lay down….get my shoes…roll over…play dead…FUCK THIS!

—Oprah the Dog

you **@peta** people need to mind ur own fuckin business… its personal shit going on here

—Oprah the Dog

About to go to the studio w/my dad tonight to make a hit record "teach you how to doggie" its gonna be hotter than the shit my dad's writing

—*Oprah the Dog*

Oprah is a miniature schnauzer. She was born in a litter of 8puppies. Just my luck I picked the only asshole

—*50 Cent*

For the last time as crazy as my dad may be he didn't break my leg. I broke that shit running after the Fed Ex man. I tried to Fly & failed

—*Oprah the Dog*

Yoko Says:

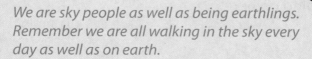

We are sky people as well as being earthlings. Remember we are all walking in the sky every day as well as on earth.

—*Yoko Ono*

#Ego

Celebrities are the greatest people on Earth. Just ask them!

I am awesome.

—Stephen Colbert

I want someone to record my voice and turn it into a font.

—John Mayer

I do NOT have to explain my resume to you my dear. However I directed 41 episodes of CIC, along with MANY other shows. **@5tephanieM**

—Scott Baio

I honestly think MORE people hate my WIFE than me… It's crazy because we're the coolest people you could ever meet…

—Ice-T

Omg I really hate chris brown #**reallymeans** I love him but I know he has things better to do with his life then worry bout my azz

—*Chris Brown*

It's great to be this handsome, but sometimes I wish I was just very good looking.

—*Michael Ian Black*

I just got compared to four loko. banned in the US. amazing. im dangerously party.

—*Ke$ha*

2 the pple who design shallow toilets. Just because u have a tiny penis doesn't mean the rest of us should have 2 dunk r junk! ;^ :-X

—*Jim Carrey*

lol i'm so smart.... :)

—*Soulja Boy*

should the SituatioN rock the sleeveless hoodie today or the guinea tee? not too sure - both lookin damn good

—*The Situation*

#CharlieSheen

After years of various scandals, Charlie Sheen's most ridiculous public meltdown started around the time he got fired from *Two and a Half Men*, started ranting insanely on talk shows, set a record for getting the most Twitter followers in a 24-hour period, and went on a tour called, "My Violent Torpedo of Truth/Defeat is Not an Option Show." Not surprisingly, he has had some interesting tweets.

#WINNING! the title of my book has finally been delivered thru vast and extensive Lunar channels. "Apocalypse Me" Warlock Latin for WINNING.

—*Charlie Sheen*

Thanks to you fabulous and perfect humans, we bludgeoned our way into the 2nd greatest book of all time. "The Guinness book" now complete.

—*Charlie Sheen*

It has all of us within it's pages. most Twitter followers EVER, 24 hr period. they should change it's title; "The Guinness Book of Us" c

—*Charlie Sheen*

this just in.... another cosmic fastball from theMind of your fav Warlock; Earn Yourself. **#EarnYourself**

—Charlie Sheen

Update: Sober Valley Lodge; Rachel has left the building...., We're sad...... Over it.... Applications now being accepted! **#winner**

—Charlie Sheen

psst, check it, you've been warned. **#SheensKorner** a violent torpedo of truth. love or hate. do the math. c

—Charlie Sheen

Dear James Franco, Your are the star of 3rd greatest movie ever made! You are also my hero! Welcome to the we've been fired hall of fame!!

—Charlie Sheen

We must bombard with Warlock Napalm, that traitor and loser whore **#DUH-neese** POOR-ards. a vile kidnapper and now dog thief. hate. SBW c

—*Charlie Sheen*

Need a ride to my perfect show.…?

—*Charlie Sheen*

Curveball; Warlock edict; pain & devastation in Japan demands us all to dig deep & LOVE THEM VIOLENTLY Dogspeed my cadres of the Far East! c

—*Charlie Sheen*

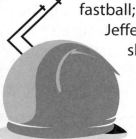

fastball; this just in, Thomas Jefferson comes forward to sheepishly admit, "Sheen's right. I am a pussy." c

—*Charlie Sheen*

Fastball; Thank you all for tuning in on an historic and victorious evening…! We did in fact, "Build the Perfect Torpedo." c

—*Charlie Sheen*

I just had Orange Juice… and CRACK for breakfast! WINNING!!!

—*Arsenio Hall*

In three days my interest in Charlie Sheen went from 0 to 60 to 0.

—*Michael Ian Black*

Making jokes about Charlie Sheen is like shooting insane fish in a barrel backed tightly with cocaine.

—*Rob Delaney*

"Do not fear.…the Sheenius is here!" I'm not gonna lie. I came back to twitter for 2 reasons. My fans and to follow **@charliesheen #winning**

—*Miley Cyrus*

@charliesheen When are you going to make an energy drink called Tiger's Blood so that we can be a nation of virile wildcats? **#sinning**

—*Eli Roth*

#AndyDickWritesAPoem

Andy Dick decided to celebrate his eleventh intervention with a poem for his fellow comedian (and colleague from their *NewsRadio* days) Kathy Griffin.

Intervention #11 last week was a real party! Thanks friends and family. Love you!

—*Andy Dick*

@kathygriffin I know you've been 'worried' so i wrote you a children's poem to let you know where i'm at.

—*Andy Dick*

@kathygriffin No more beer, no more wine, I was intervened on by friends of mine.

—*Andy Dick*

@kathygriffin But i can still party, and i can still dance, and lil' andy dick will stay in my pants.

—*Andy Dick*

#TyraBanks

Like Larry King, Tyra Banks is a celebrity who is just looking for answers to life's questions—how would my name sound with an Italian accent? What nontraditional scent do I want to smell like right now? What kind of nose-picking do I prefer? Deep stuff.

BellyButton talk time! I used to be outtie, now I'm innie. Weird. Maybe I am an alien… U outtie or innie? N how often u clean it?

—Tyra Banks

Strawberry sundae topping. Doubles as a good blush for my cheeks. What other food would be good makeup?

—Tyra Banks

It kinda sounds like "Tyyyyyy-rhah……" How would your name sound with an Italian accent?

—Tyra Banks

Ok guys, here's one for you: Which would u choose? A girl who dug in her nose all the time or a girl who dug in YOUR nose all the time?

—*Tyra Banks*

If u could spray yourself with a non typical scent right now, what would it be???

—*Tyra Banks*

Yoko Says:

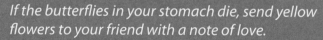

If the butterflies in your stomach die, send yellow flowers to your friend with a note of love.

—*Yoko Ono*

#LindsayLohan

Lindsay Lohan is no stranger to drama, whether it's bickering with her d-bag dad after he leaks voice mail messages from her or arguing with her on-again, off-again girlfriend, Samantha Ronson.

[link to music video] that was for my ex-father

—*Lindsay Lohan*

@LindsayLohan…you sing of LOVE & I speak of LOVE BEING sacrifice. I proved it over and over & I am willing to prove it now, 2 help & save you

—*Michael Lohan*

@LindsayLohan…who WENT TO JAIL for 2 yrs because U and mom cried 2 me 2 come to LA, while I was on Probation, knowing I'd get violated? ME!

—*Michael Lohan*

@LindsayLohan…How about the briefcases of money I'd give you, mom and the kids to spend? Who flew back and forth every week, Coast to coast

—Michael Lohan

@LindsayLohan… was I wrong for yelling. YES, but how about all the things mom did? remember Atlantis? Remember the lies to the cops?

—Michael Lohan

My father just sent me this as I was leaving the gym "I told you to stop Linds this is the last time…

—Lindsay Lohan

and take down the tweet about me HURTING MOM… U will be getting a call from SOMEBODY today to end you"

—Lindsay Lohan

@LindsayLohan… YOU R TWISTING THINGS JUST LIKE THE MEDIA DOES. THE VERY PEOPLE U CRITICIZE

—Michael Lohan

@LindsayLohan …I never said that. I have it on my text (it is date and time stamped)! what is wrong with U OOOPS! I already 1 know that

—Michael Lohan

Lindsay Lohan is so dumb. Her idea of being sworn in is cursing at the judge.

—Joan Rivers

Joan Rivers and her "stargument" make me believe that she and Michael Lohan are a match made in heaven……

—Lindsay Lohan

.…all he needs is her botox doctor. "Dr." Drew- any ideas? Botox rehab reality show?

—Lindsay Lohan

in the words of 50 cent… "You shouldn't throw stones if you live in a glass house and if you got a glass jaw, you should watch yo mouth"

—Lindsay Lohan

Thanks **@lindsaylohan** sounds like a terrific plan! Actually happy to see you have retained your sense of humor despite your circumstances

—Dr. Drew

the only "bookings" that i'm familiar with are Disney Films, never thought that i'd be "booking" into Jail.… eeeks

—Lindsay Lohan

@lindsaylohan well- you haven't lost your sense of humour.

—Samantha Ronson

Yoko Says:

The invisible room: Everybody should have one.

—Yoko Ono

#RobDelaney

Rob Delaney is a stand-up comedian who has found a special niche as a Twitter comic. Apparently that's a thing now.

My friend's baby looks like a shitty drawing of a baby.

—*Rob Delaney*

Draw a picture of a house. Congratulations; you're an architect. I don't know what the fuss is about those assholes.

—*Rob Delaney*

MAKE-A-WISH FOUNDATION REP: "So you just want a chubby Jewish girl to sit on your lap while you smell her hair for 5 hours?" ME: "Correct."

—*Rob Delaney*

When someone apologizes because their dog is barking at me, I say, "It's okay; he just senses I'm going to kill him tonight."

—*Rob Delaney*

From now on if something is super crazy, say it's "Wackaroni & Jeez!" Can you even handle it? I know! So fun.…

—*Rob Delaney*

I think it would be fun to watch vegan college students rationalize eating roadkill during the Apocalypse.

—*Rob Delaney*

Have you ever cut open a pepper & found a little baby pepper inside it & then gotten sad & missed your mom?

—*Rob Delaney*

If someone is VERY white or VERY black, I assume they have magic powers.

—*Rob Delaney*

Children give terrible gifts because they're poor.

—*Rob Delaney*

Tough guys who wear sunglasses on the back of their head are covering their "gay eyes" that are checking out other dudes' dongs.

—*Rob Delaney*

This is going to sound like a generalization, but all people who drive white pickup trucks are rapists.

—*Rob Delaney*

If you don't like one of my tweets, rearrange the letters into something you do like. I can't wipe your ass for you.

—*Rob Delaney*

Watching my wife arrange pillows on our couch makes Rain Man look like Tommy Boy.

—*Rob Delaney*

I like it when corporations have a sassy "human" Twitter presence, like their CEO wouldn't cut your mom's throat for a nickel.

—*Rob Delaney*

Yoko Says:

Imagine the eternity you will be living in. Smile! I love you!!!

—*Yoko Ono*

#Snooki&Pals

The cast of *Jersey Shore* tweet about their favorite things: tanning, partying…and themselves. It's "exuberating."

Omg tanning for the first time in 2 months!!! This is going to be exuberating! (Hope I used that right lmao) **#givemeprops**

—*Snooki*

---

saw a woman that looked like snookie at the gym. apparently not the best compliment to be called a snook-alike. o well, live and learn…

—*David Spade*

....

@DavidSpade She must be buggin. Just sayeennnn.

—*Snooki*

On the streets in the city randomly spray tanning peoples faces with SunLove, haha yes!

—Snooki

You have jus excluded yourself from SUrf n Turf NIght- you are also excluded from ravioli night n not to mention chicken cutlet night –SItch

—The Situation

Getting ready for Leno in my white paradise hotel room.… Watch your bronzers as you enter please.

—Snooki

Diva? i don't think so - i'm like a Ferrari - i'm hi maintenance but i go fast and look good - KinG of QuOTES - SiTCh - GTL

—The Situation

Going to bail **@Sn00ki** out of jail.… The things I do for this girl I swear.

—*JWoww*

Even when im 80, ill still be burnt toast tan, with my poof in the nursin home searchin for gweeds with **@jenniwoww.**

—*Snooki*

GTL-SItch- in Cali doing it big- said it from the beginning- lol if hatin is your OCcupation- I prob got a full time job for yah! SItuation

—*The Situation*

Valentines day is the hardest day of the year fo a playa – shiiiieeettttt

—*Vinny Guadagnino*

I found a new bronzer that does wonders! very satisfied right now

—*Snooki*

Ok Life is Complete, I Just Fist Pumped With Goofy @ Magic Kingdom!!!!

—Pauly D

Space Mountain Was Serious!!!!! And My BlowOut Didnt Even Move!!!!

—Pauly D

ill show you bitches whats up

—Snooki

Airports give me anxiety! I suggest they put in ever airport a club, a nail salon and a tanning salon so I could relieve all this stress

—Snooki

Just did an interview for the uk and let me tell ya I friggin love their accents! Ellow my british gweedows

—Snooki

Omg this car just lifted off the ground goin over this hill and squished my poof on the roof. Almost had a heart attack. Whew....

—*Snooki*

I need a day dedicated to the nair salon, hair salon, tanning salon, gym, spa and shopping. I need me a fun lovin snooki assistant Lol!!

—*Snooki*

Feeding these Haters steaming alpo cause I'm dogging em on a daily basis! Situation nation gtl reality legend! Keep hat in, not goin anywher

—*The Situation*

I love being tan.

—*Snooki*

#Boozing

It's a well-known fact that celebrities are boozers. They handle intoxication with the grace and elegance you would expect.

What the shiballs! My cognac is almost gone!

—Danny DeVito

Slow tweet day because of early onset cocktail hour.

—Steve Martin

Drunken HUNT FOR RED OCTOBER

—Alec Baldwin

Drunken HUNT FOR RED OCTOBER test…..… Say "Magneto-hydrodynamic drive" three times fast. With a Scottish accent.

—Alec Baldwin

Friend told me today not to drink and tweet.

—*Alec Baldwin*

God did not make liquor! Man is an evil thing to make some shit to make u feel so good then so damn bad. Will I ever shit again???

—*Marlon Wayans*

I am going to a scrap booking party tonight LOL! I will get drunk for Sure!

—*Lisa Rinna*

I'm not just sayin this because I'm drunk but I fucking love you guys. You are like, my best friends! I'm gonna lie down in the coat room.

—*Simon Pegg*

I WOULD LIKE A HAMBURGER WIT ERRRR THANG ON IT.....................hold the mayo

—*Juicy J*

Icecold public toliet ring worm sandwhich face ass!

—*Juicy J*

Hey bruh jus leavin a bar & i'm drunk as a fool hahHHahaahahaahabaabbabbababaa babbababababbaababababbababababaababa baab

—*Juicy J*

Gooooon morin! Went to a house party last nite how the fuk did I get home I cant remeber shit! Hahahahaha my head is killin me!

—*Juicy J*

#SteveMartin

Steve Martin, the former king of Hollywood comedies, is now a banjo-strumming bluegrass star who tweets constantly.

Starting a massive new media campaign to promote the idea that I am "famously shy."
—*Steve Martin*

A very good gardener I know just told me my ass is grass. Nice compliment.
—*Steve Martin*

STEVE MARTIN IS REALLY OILED AND BUFF. OMG, my Twitter account was just hacked.
—*Steve Martin*

If you lean in real close, this tweet smells of lavender.
—*Steve Martin*

I've decided I want to get to know Cher on a first name basis.

—*Steve Martin*

I'm wasting my time trying to come up with a good tweet, so, out of anger, I'm going to waste your time by having you read this one.

—*Steve Martin*

From Steve's Compendium of Strange and Little Known Facts: The baskets for the basketball playoffs are NOT woven by Navajos.

—*Steve Martin*

BAD DOG! (sometimes it helps if it comes from someone they've seen on TV)

—*Steve Martin*

I think it was Abraham Lincoln who said, "I want to get x-rays to prove my butt's real."
—*Steve Martin*

Currently feeding data into computer to determine whether or not today is a beautiful day. Will keep you posted.
—*Steve Martin*

Yoko Says:

Think of your room as a prison. Make the best of it and be proud of it. Think of your room as a castle. Invite people and share the joy.

—*Yoko Ono*

#AndrewWKJustWants EveryoneToParty,OK?

Andrew WK is a rock star who just really wants everyone to stop what they're doing right now and party with him. Is that so wrong?

PARTY TIP: Think about how intense it is to be a woman.

—Andrew WK

PARTY TIP: When your friends come over, offer them a sliced radish, egg, or steak. Then put the music on!

—Andrew WK

PARTY TIP: I humbly request that you gently approach all small young dogs like basic soft angels.

—Andrew WK

If God didn't want us to party, he wouldn't have invented me!

—*Andrew WK*

PARTY TIP: Smile more often. It looks awesome.

—*Andrew WK*

PARTY TIP: Think how amazing it is that life exists at all! It's a total miracle that we get to be here! PARTY out of respect!

—*Andrew WK*

PARTY TIP: Don't feel the need to invite me to your party – I'm already coming! In fact, I'm already there! And I'm puking!

—*Andrew WK*

IT'S WEDNESDAY. IT'S TIME TO PARTY. DEAL WITH IT.

—*Andrew WK*

If you hate your job, I want you to quit TODAY. Tell your boss, "Andrew WK told me to!" Then report back to me so we can party.

—*Andrew WK*

If you don't party, your stories are probably boring and probably end with, "And then I got home."

—*Andrew WK*

PARTY TIP: You weren't actually thinking of giving up on your dreams, were you?

—*Andrew WK*

PARTY TIP: Don't be mean today.

—*Andrew WK*

#Groan

Cheesy celebrity jokes ahoy!

Don't say I'm not hip. I'm very hip, in fact, I had a new one put in, and it's made me even hipper.

—*John Cleese*

Plan on seeing my miracle working chiropractor if she can fit me in today. She really cracks me up!….Oooh, they can't all be gems!

—*Lou Diamond Phillips*

There is no astronaut training for celebrity.… even though this whole life is so outer space!

—*Kanye West*

I could never do stand up cause I tell jokes better when I'm sitting

—*Kanye West*

I once owned a pair of glasses so big, I had to clean them with a squeegee!

—*Larry King*

It's a good day to reflect. I'm laying out in my back yard wrapped in aluminum foil.

—*Bob Saget*

#SarahSilverman

Sarah Silverman is a comedian, author, and actress. Yet she seems a little obsessed with her maid's bathroom habits.

Life is so short! I'm gonna watch every possible episode of Law&Order while I'm strong and healthy!

—*Sarah Silverman*

When my dog yawns it smells like all the farts in the world took a shit. But do I still love him? No.

—*Sarah Silverman*

I live in a tiny 3 room apt but still when my housekeeper comes she eats a meal &takes a shit

—*Sarah Silverman*

I wish I was as comfortable with my body as I want young girls to think I am.
—*Sarah Silverman*

Elderly woman in line to board plane turned around and blew a long silent powerful burp onto my face
—*Sarah Silverman*

Gotta respect my housekeeper for leaving her shit scrapes in my toilet. It's pretty gangster.
—*Sarah Silverman*

Had my first long bike ride - wow! - It was like flying! Like flying while getting punched in the vagina!
—*Sarah Silverman*

Yoko Says:

Imagine running across a wheat field as fast as you can. Imagine your friend running towards you as fast as possible.

—Yoko Ono

#Drama

Nothing beats some awkward celebrity drama, whether it's Kim Kardashian versus Demi Moore, or musician Aimee Mann versus Ice-T. But you have to feel for Frances Bean Cobain, the seemingly sensible daughter of Courtney Love and the late Kurt Cobain, who valiantly tries to rein in her mother's rants.

GOT A COMPLAINT? Take it up with Dave Grohl, whose financed his mom and his entire families properties (exes too) with "Nirvana"$Kurt$!

—Courtney Love

i'm relieving you from twitter duties. go watch madmen&turn off the computer. put it down…nice&slow. easy. easy. good!

—Frances Bean Cobain

LAtely Madonnas been very passive agressiveky mean to me making mutual friends take sides, kaboshing plans i had

—Courtney Love

someone adopt me please?

—Frances Bean Cobain

Someone that has no meaning in my life tweeted something sh*tty about me just now. I tweeted back. then erased it. I'm above it.

—*Jenna Jameson*

I do want to say this... I NEVER turned my back on porn. I moved on, unlike some people that are 45 and still doing it, which is sad.

—*Jenna Jameson*

Big pimpin w **@SerenaJWilliams @LalaVazquez**

—*Kim Kardashian*

Are you using the word "pimpin" as in pimping? RT**@KimKardashian**: Big pimpin w **@SerenaJWilliams @LalaVazquez**

—*Demi Moore*

@[Demi Moore] Nothing wrong with dancing to Big Pimpin' by Jay Z in the club! Having a girls night out, gotta love that song!

—*Kim Kardashian*

@KimKardashian No disrespect I love a girls night out but a pimp and pimping is nothing more than a slave owner!

—*Demi Moore*

Ok, trying to move on to funny twats now…What celebrity should I get in to a Twitter war with? Jealous of Kim K vs Demi Moore.

—*Kathy Griffin*

Christ, there is no reason in the world anyone should ever have cast Ice-T in a television show.

—*Aimee Mann*

Hey **@aimeemann** stop worrying bout my acting bitch, and worry about your WACK ass music. In the mean time… Eat a hot bowl of Dicks! Ice-T

—*Ice-T*

Oh NOOOO!! Someone just told me that Ice-T responded to my tweet about him!! THIS CAN'T BE GOOD!!!

—*Aimee Mann*

I am not going to read it. I DO NOT WANT HIM MAD AT ME!!

—*Aimee Mann*

He's out there doing his job. He doesn't need any heckling from the peanut gallery. So, I am sorry, Mr. T! You get out there and DO IT!

—*Aimee Mann*

OK. Homegirl apologized……. Say no more FLTG Cease fire! "Once again there's Peace in Twitterland." Ice-T

—*Ice-T*

Thanks 4 watching everyone. I know I had a good night when I wake up with tape on my back & glitter on my face. Now, I have to go do my show

—*Chelsea Handler*

@RyanSeacrest I think you should host the VMAs next year! Or ME! Ha! We both would have done a better job than Chelsea did!

—*Perez Hilton*

@perezhilton oh, fuck off. I had a blast and the show awesome last night. Bomb? Your life is a bomb.

—*Chelsea Handler*

@chelseahandler At least I didn't have to fuck my way to a talk show and sleep with the head of the network. **#TedHarbert**

—*Perez Hilton*

@chelseahandler And who'd you blow to get the VMA hosting gig? I'm more than happy with my bomb life. It's da bomb.com! xo

—*Perez Hilton*

I'll always say what I really feel. And I don't have to sit behind a computer screen to do it. I'll tell you to your face!

—*Perez Hilton*

Just got word....Highest rated vma's since 2002. Good job, mtv! Good job, kiddo.
—*Chelsea Handler*

Donald Trump is a Pompous Asshole! Saw him in Aspen with one Dcup chick after another Everyone up there thought he was a complete idiot
—*Cher*

Pls retweet! Donald Trump (mr chapter11) is Only a Mean Spirited BAD ACTOR who couldn't find his ass with both hands & a map !
—*Cher*

Yoko Says:

Get a telephone that only echoes back your voice. Call every day and complain and moan about your life and people around you.
—*Yoko Ono*

#JohnMayer

John Mayer, a singer who became tabloid fodder after dating Jessica Simpson and Jennifer Aniston, was a prolific Twit until he deleted his account after a controversial *Playboy* interview.

Taking a black friend to do some shopping at Reparation Hardware.

—*John Mayer*

My mouth is the Don King of my penis.

—*John Mayer*

Dear Carl's Jr, I told myself that if I saw you on my drive I would do you. I would do you hard. But you didn't show.

—*John Mayer*

I'm with brown rice and chicken now. Not as hot, but it was there for me. And it wants me. And that means something right now.

—*John Mayer*

Look, just because it itches doesn't mean it stinks.

—*John Mayer*

Whenever they say it cant be done, remind them that they make a jellybean that tastes exactly like popcorn.

—*John Mayer*

#StephenColbert

Stephen Colbert had the most re-tweeted message of 2010, saying after the BP oil spill that "in honor of oil-soaked birds, 'tweets' are now 'gurgles.'" He continues his hilarity daily, and calls his Twitter followers "Colbert Nation."

When meeting royalty, it is very important, no matter how excited you are, not to vomit on them. Instead, vomit on the nearest commoner.

—*Stephen Colbert*

When life gives you lemons, go ahead and whip them right back at life. I mean, come on. Enough with the lemons already.

—*Stephen Colbert*

For Christmas this year I gave half my staff iPads and the other half switchblades. Let's see what happens!

—*Stephen Colbert*

( )( ).… Oh no! I think I just accidentally tweeted an emoticon of my ass! **#ivebeenhacked**

—*Stephen Colbert*

I've got an ace in the hole. I just can't figure out how to get it out. Does anyone have really tiny fingers?

—*Stephen Colbert*

Even after all those etiquette lessons, I'm still not sure which fork to throw at my butler when his thumb touches my plate.

—*Stephen Colbert*

Part of me wonders if the inside of a pig's mouth constantly tastes like bacon. And the other part says I don't need to test that again.

—*Stephen Colbert*

If I had a hammer, I'd hammer in the morning. But honestly, by evening, I'd probably move onto something like sawing.

—*Stephen Colbert*

When people notice my scar, I say 'you should have seen the other guy,' because it's true - I cut that surgeon really badly.

—*Stephen Colbert*

If I had a nickel for every time I said "If I had a nickel," I'd have 2 nickels. I don't say it much.

—*Stephen Colbert*

Yoko Says:

Once we were told that God created us in his image. Now we can duplicate ourselves in OUR image in millions from one cell in our hair.

—*Yoko Ono*

#Someone'sAngry!

Some celebrities just want to vent, even if it makes them sound a little unbalanced.

Bottom line "DO NOT F**K WITH ME, MY FAMILY OR MY NON PROFIT" Ur 3rd grade politics IS OVER, GROW UP. Ur NOT a xmen superhero use ur real nm

—Scott Baio

And if you don't like what i'm saying, UNFOLLOW ME U STUPID ASS. that simple. Get money

—Soulja Boy

I'm sick of lame liars! You are not flattering anybody… Uh

—Mary-Kate Olsen

"Tip of the day: don't ever get married, its a nightmare, and everyone involved (or not as the case may be) turns into a c**t."

—*Lily Allen*

Funny how you find out you were just a promotion vehicle to someone. It's pathetic.

—*Brooke Hogan*

my ex boyfriend is a tool.

—*Ricki Lake*

Listen up fat fuck as a real northerner I was brought up 2 say shit 2 people's faces not behind their back. Live forever LG

—*Liam Gallagher*

YOU ALL NEED TO SHUT UP. I DONT HAVE A BOYFRIIEND < I DONT WANT A BOYFRIEND I DONT NEED A BOYFRIEND AND ALL YOU DO IS FUCK W KIDS! STOP IT NOW!

—*Courtney Love*

I'll never take a gift from anyone… This way I can tell anyone to f***off anytime…

—*Mike Tyson*

Actors are just the bestest people in thw world! We are so lucky to be sharing the earth with them!! Fuck!!!

—*Bill Maher*

I'm unhappy with Christian Scientists! U say U love your kids while U let them suffer and rott! There's no Christ in neglect. So F*ck U! ;^)

—*Jim Carrey*

SOME OF YALL ACT LIKE IF THE MAN DONT ATTEND THEN HE DOESNT CARE! THAT TOTALLY NOT IT!!I LOVE MY SON AND DAUGHTER UNCONDITIONALLY!

—Nelly

A middle finger is more New York than a corporate ambush. I bleed for my hometown, and I'd die for my fans.

—Lady Gaga

Honestly, The National Enquirer is so full of ca ca…with this "Star wants to marry Al again" story. Please quit trippin. **#CompleteLIE**

—Star Jones

Call me fat, call me skelator, call me a bobble head…but don't make up TOTALLY false crap. I haven't even SPOKEN to Al since June 2007!

—Star Jones

Dang…I'm all mad…now I have to go to a lunch meeting and smile. Let me put these lashes on and get out of here. I hope they have wine!

—*Star Jones*

Being scolded by a GOSSIP SHOW for talking about people's personal lives is like a turd saying ya smell bad! No offense to actual turds! ;^\

—*Jim Carrey*

Dear tabloid media aka FILTH: pls note I expressed an overall feeling bout product placement, their roles in vids & the art of them being…

—*Katy Perry*

complimenting or sticking out. Most, if not ALL popsters welcome deals w/products 2 offset costs of big budget vids in these recessional…

—*Katy Perry*

music industry times. I'VE used them in MY vids before & am happy 2b able 2 make a better vid because of. Once AGAIN, stop pitting artists…

—*Katy Perry*

against artist for ur sensational satisfaction & stick to what ur best @: lying gossiping, exaggerating & overall lending a hand 2 the…

—*Katy Perry*

…deterioration of a generation.

—*Katy Perry*

I'm a 23 year old rockstar with NO KIDS! What's up with everybody wantin me to be a parent? I'm justa girl, I can only be your/our voice!

—*Rihanna*

And this is why! Cuz we turn the other cheek! U can't hide your kids from society, or they'll never learn how to adapt! This is the REAL WORLD!

—*Rihanna*

Cuz we all know how difficult/embarrassing it is to communicate touchy subject matters to anyone especially our parents!

—*Rihanna*

The music industry isn't exactly Parents R Us! We have the freedom to make art, LET US! Its your job to make sure they dont turn out like US

—*Rihanna*

People gon' talk whether u doin BAD or GOOD!!! Yeeeaaaaaaaa

—*Rihanna*

If it weren't for twitter i'd never know what anyone said about or thought of me. WOW i'd be so happy and free!

—*Joel Madden*

There is a MISCONCEPTION that CELEBRITIES don't work. That's some stank bullshit! Our job is 24 hours a day. The hourly sucks

—*Marlon Wayans*

IM SO TIRED OF LAME AZZ PEOPLE… UUGGGGGHHH>>lol

—*Chris Brown*

Yoko Says:

Take your pants off before you fight.

—*Yoko Ono*

#TomHanksHadSomeWeird PredictionsFor2011

…and he shared them on Twitter.

In 2011.… I predict we will watch TV on small, hand-help screens called 'Tele-bits'. What a wonder that will be! Hanx
—*Tom Hanks*

In the year 2011 telegrams will be replaced by a device called the twit-o-gram and cost only pennies. Amazing! Hanx
—*Tom Hanks*

In the year 2011.…TV will have over 30 Channels! Some, in other languages! How amazing will THAT be! Hanx
—*Tom Hanks*

In the year 2011 foods from all over Asia will be available in the USA, anytime, anywhere. Incredible! Hanx
—*Tom Hanks*

#WordsAreHard

Celebrities are not known for their spelling and grammar, but there's something extra fun about Jessica Simpson misspelling "dweeb" when talking about her poor spelling.

on my last day in Morocco i have finally learned it is spelled with 2 c's and not 2 r's. I am a dweb!! i mean REALLY?!?! :)
— *Jessica Simpson*

Why is that people always try to understand estimate my intelligents?! They should never do that! I haven't been on (cont)
— *Mary J Blige*

So Sorry for my miss spelling of the word Intelligence. Thanks for checking me. This is how we learn.
— *Mary J Blige*

Ok, fine, but what about "understand estimate" and "miss spelling"? Sigh.

I love how everyone says "its a no brainer" were the "no brainer generation"

—*Pete Wentz*

And the no-apostrophe generation, too, by the looks of it.

---

just finnished wrighting my closer column!

—*Kelly Osbourne*

"Finnished wrighting," you say?

Leonard Bernstein is the shit!!! Hit flute player is snapping write now!!!

—*Kanye West*

Leonard Bernstein is dead. right now. RT **@kanyewest** Leonard Bernstein is the shit!!! Hit flute player is snapping write now!!!

—*Jimmy Kimmel*

Hello Teittaverse hops all is well out there
—*John Cusack*

Thank God they are making ANOTHER Superman movie! And people say creaitivity is dead in Hollywood.
—*Jim Gaffigan*

Dear Twitter police, I didn't misspell "creative". I spelled it creatively.
—*Jim Gaffigan*

Da next niga 2 korrect my spellin gone get killed You fuck boys no how we do in da south lol brrr
—*50 Cent*

Yoko Says:

The gallery space returned to peace when I wrapped a bunch of celeries instead.
—*Yoko Ono*

#SpencerAndHeidi

Spencer Pratt and Heidi Montag, former stars of *The Hills*, love-love-love them some attention. They'll say and do anything for a little publicity—from undergoing ten plastic surgeries in one day (Heidi) to blabbering about crystals and meditation (Spencer). They even appeared on *I'm a Celebrity, Get Me Out of Here*, feuding with anyone who even glanced their way, much as they do on Twitter.

I take back the quote that I am the white Jay Z! I did my research I am nothing like this person so please forget I ever said this! Thanks!

—Spencer Pratt

@**ryanseacrest** is a testament that any poser wanna be loser can have success in Hollywood!

—Spencer Pratt

@**ryanseacrest** I CAN'T WAIT to see you face to face! Your going to pee and poop in your pants when you see my eyes!

—Spencer Pratt

@RyanSeacrest is discusting!

—*Heidi Montag*

My Mage has informed me that the universe wants me to entertain the world and not be President of the United States. What a relief!

—*Spencer Pratt*

I have proven that KUNDALINI YOGA taps your Feminine power in your body because I find myself crying now at least once a day!

—*Spencer Pratt*

My dream is to star in the remake of Splash directed by Ron Howard! Please help my wish to come true be send all you loving energy! love you

—*Heidi Montag*

I would like to make it CLEAR! My wife and audrina have severed all ties! We no longer deal with that fake world and fake people like her.

—*Spencer Pratt*

Audrina – Don't hate because your nasty Tijuana plastic surgery got you no press… and my wife is #1 story on people – 5 days in a row!

—*Spencer Pratt*

So glad my wife gets her surgery in bev hills and not where Jwow and audrina go. We love american doctors!

—*Spencer Pratt*

Ke$ha on SNL this week – looks like a dragon on E threw up on a super hero outfit.

—*Spencer Pratt*

"Michael Bay I love your work! I know what a artistic brilliant genius you are! Cast me in the next Transformers."

—*Heidi Montag*

My last surgery was the BEST decision of my life! Anything else anyone says (family members who are trying to make money off of me) is a lie!

—*Heidi Montag*

I have never felt sexier, happier, or more amazing in my own skin. I truly look the way I have always dreamed, I love America and freedom!

—*Heidi Montag*

Douche is a compliment to me. It cleans a magical place with loving care.

—*Spencer Pratt*

America loves a good comeback.

—*Spencer Pratt*

Ok, I've made a decision. Hey **@Heidimontag**, you do not appear to be very intelligent. Also, your husband looks a little "date rape-y".

—*Kathy Griffin*

Yoko Says:

The human race is in its embryonic stage.

—*Yoko Ono*

#Let'sGetIt

Rapper Nelly really likes breakfast food.

pancakes!!!!! LETS GET IT

—Nelly

TURKY BACON!!! LETS GET IT!!

—Nelly

SCRAMBLE EGGS WIT CHEESE!!! LET GET IT!!

—Nelly

OATMEAL!! LETS GET IT!!!

—Nelly

#Cher

Cher tweets! Yes, that Cher! She's all piss and vinegar—
and randomly capitalized WORDS!

2 Much ? 2 out there 4 an OLD CHICK !
U MIGHT SAY ?!! Too €%%¥+€<#

—Cher

•= ing BAD !

—Cher

We didn't get a nomination 4
best song ! That sucks! Diane's
song Is so beautiful! It's hard to
understand how u win

—Cher

The Golden Globe 4 BEST SONG
& not even get nominated by
the OSCARS? Oh well it is…
what it is ,,,,the sun is still
shining !

—Cher

Some A.H. Said "Cher Gripes about not getting nominated 4 "U haven't seen the last of me " However.… so far NO ONE has had to say t …

—Cher

HER……Would u like Some Cheese 2 go with that WHINE!"

—Cher

To Say to me .… " Excuse me CHER.… Would you like some Cheese to go With that Whine? & SO Whatever your name is…

—Cher

E LACK OF RESPECT & TOTAL DISREGARD Up Yours Dude ! xxxxCHER

—Cher

Whatever Your Name Is?? It is With TOTAL Disregard & Complete Lack Of respect…… That i Wish u Goodnight & Goodfknluck xxxxCher !

—Cher

One thing. Didn't Know caps were shouting! I'm SO out of the loop. Probably out of the loop Is outta the loop

—*Cher*

People romanticize u when you're Gone

—*Cher*

THANK GOD!

—*Cher*

#PattonOswalt

Patton Oswalt is a comedian who was Remy in *Ratatouille*, Spence on *King of Queens*, and Neil on the *United States of Tara*. But he might be best known for his bit about KFC's famous bowls—as well as his funny tweets.

The hipster using a cane who doesn't need said cane just spilled his coffee because of said cane. YES.

—Patton Oswalt

Someone on this plane a) just farted and b) eats a lot of granola bars.

—Patton Oswalt

The "this vehicle has been checked for sleeping children" signs on schoolbuses exist because of a scary & hilarious incident.

—Patton Oswalt

Wait, at the end of "Shout", the singer tells everyone to, "Take it easy." Hey asshole, you're the one that riled us up.

—*Patton Oswalt*

I've caught the kind of cold where my body feels like a skid row hotel full of puking junkies.

—*Patton Oswalt*

I always refer to "air conditioning" as "climate control" 'cuz then it sounds like a superpower.

—*Patton Oswalt*

I hope my obituary headline includes the words "runs amok".

—*Patton Oswalt*

#CelebPals

With all the Hollywood drama and name-dropping on Twitter, it's just nice to see celebrities who actually know (and like) each other and don't mind all of Twitterdom to know about it. It's especially refreshing when they're actually funny, like Will Arnett (*Arrested Development*) and Brit Simon Pegg (*Shaun of the Dead*).

Ahh, to be back in the sweet, loving embrace of London.…I hope this city's not a dude.
—*Will Arnett*

@**arnettwill** woah woah woah, who let you in?!
—*Simon Pegg*

@**simonpegg** Kevin. Lives in Wembley with his mum.…Vim under the sink.…you know.…Kevin!
—*Will Arnett*

@**arnettwill** Oh yeah, Kev. I've got his Sex and the City box set. Can you let him know? Thanks love. x
—*Simon Pegg*

@simonpegg he said "he's fine wif dat"… we're currently trying to scrub some butterscotch off his jumper

—*Will Arnett*

@arnettwill That is soooo Kevin. That and fingering sheep.

—*Simon Pegg*

Well everyone, I'm off to the gym. It's entirely too early for exercise.

—*Paula Deen*

@paula_deen paula i'm off to the gym too, can we get together make some biscuits friend chicken the works then go work out please!

—*Sandra Bernhard*

I just tried Almond Milk today…thanks **@nicolerichie** for the health food tip!

—*Kim Kardashian*

@KimKardashian no prob bob. theres 1 side effect where you grow a tiny little penis, but I'm sure you wont mind. Enjoy!

—*Nicole Richie*

Not a drop of gasoline! All electric car! Drive all LA, plug it in, drive some more. Not a drop of gas @ 3.99 a gall.…

—*Tom Hanks*

@tomhanks But Tom, you can afford 3,000 mile plug. The rest of us can't.

—*Steve Martin*

@kirstiealley I have a no make out policy with guests. I've only broken it once (with Regis) so who knows… brush your teeth xxx

—*Craig Ferguson*

ahhh!! Got the @**jimmykimmel** curse and my radio computers crashed! We just bolted from my E! studio to our backup studio at @**1027kiisfm**

—*Ryan Seacrest*

I am so sorry Ryan. Had I known I was infectious, I would not have called. Fortunately, hair gel is a natural antibiotic @**RyanSeacrest**

—*Jimmy Kimmel*

About to get on a plane to Chile. Special thanks to James Franco for finding my Dad's bookmark, otherwise we'd still be looking for it.

—*Eli Roth*

James Franco finding my Dad's bookmark was a Hollywood moment. My mom then asking "Who's James Franco?" was a Cora Roth moment.

—*Eli Roth*

@rihanna yo batch lemme borrow those latex dresses! **#slutty #skank #ho #whore #bearcunt #yesyesyes!**

—*Katy Perry*

ur a role model, u can't use those words!! **#appalled** lol!! RT **@katyperry**: **#slutty #skank #ho #whore #bearcunt #yesyesyes!**

—*Rihanna*

@conanobrien forced to tweet against my will by book publisher. help me.

—*Albert Brooks*

Sorry **@AlbertBrooks**, you are beyond help. You're on Twitter, and nobody under 25 knows what a "book" is.

—*Conan O'Brien*

Yoko Says:

Each planet has its own orbit agenda. Think of people close to you as planets. Sometimes it's nice to just watch them orbit and shine.

—Yoko Ono

#SarahPalin

Regardless of what you think of Sarah Palin politically, it's hard to take any politician seriously when they refuse to use actual sentences.

Earth saw clmate chnge4 ions; will cont 2 c chnges. R duty2responsbly devlop resorces4humankind/not pollute&destroy; but cant alter naturl chng

—*Sarah Palin*

"2 PA school speech; I'll intro kids 2 beauty of laissez-faire via serving them cookies amidst school cookie ban debate; Nanny state run amok!"

—*Sarah Palin*

Commonsense Conservaties & lovers of America: "Don't Retreat, Instead – RELOAD!" Pls see my Facebook page.

—*Sarah Palin*

Extreme Greenies: see now why we push "drill,baby,drill" of known reserves&promising finds in safe onshore places like ANWR? Now do you get it?

—*Sarah Palin*

Who hijacked term: "feminist"? A cackle of rads who want 2 crucify other women w/ whom they disagree on a singular issue; it's ironic (& passé)

—*Sarah Palin*

Wow, media goofballs rearing heads this wk, big time! Wonder what's up? Taking the cake: ink re: Bristol=a diva? Silly; obviously have nvr met her

—*Sarah Palin*

#JoanRivers

Joan Rivers on Twitter is much like Joan Rivers on TV, or on stage, or wherever else you see her: a mix of mean and funny.

Miley Cyrus and her mother offend white trash.

—*Joan Rivers*

I have absolutely no sex appeal! My sex life is like the Soviet Union – it ended 19 years ago!

—*Joan Rivers*

It's February 3rd, which can only mean one thing. Eleven days until men ignore me for the 77th Valentine's Day in a row.

—*Joan Rivers*

Depressed thinking about my birthday. Do you know how bad it feels to have your life flash before your eyes and it takes 6 and ½ hours?

—*Joan Rivers*

Happy Groundhog Day! This morning I emerged from a plastic surgeon's office, saw my shadow and realized I needed to have my nose done again.

—*Joan Rivers*

Finding it sad and difficult to write an obituary for a friend who died over the weekend. Is it wrong to say he loved black men and pizza?

—*Joan Rivers*

When you get older, you find pleasure in different things. Like today, I'm walking around in a clean diaper!

—*Joan Rivers*

My body's so terrible, Sports Illustrated asked me to be in their Snowsuit Issue.

—*Joan Rivers*

#TooMuchInformation

Celebrities often share way too much personal information with their legions of Twitter followers. For example, actress Lisa Rinna has a secret weapon for happiness in her marriage to actor Harry Hamlin—a secret weapon we probably don't need to know about.

it is time for khloe to put mayonnaise on my vjine since i can barely see that thing with this baby bump. night night beautiful twitterfam!

—*Kourtney Kardashian*

my dickhead is shaped liked a darth vadar helmet. my dick is so fat it looks like r2d2.

—*Tracy Morgan*

Freshly waxed and ready for summer. Also, I'm free-balling for the first time ever today. **#newtraditions**

—*Johnny Weir*

I think it was me who said, "Boredom is for those who are afraid to masterbate." G'night folks! ;^)

—*Jim Carrey*

Of course, I meant "masturbate' in my last tweet! I spell it 'masterbate' because I happen to have mastered it! ;^o

—*Jim Carrey*

Bout to put my head between this girl legs at my crib

—*Soulja Boy*

I only wax. I have never shaved

—*Khloe Kardashian*

The Key to a lasting marriage in Hollywood. Good Porn.

—Lisa Rinna

Truth be told I like Vivid the best

—Lisa Rinna

I would recommend the Colace brand to anyone looking for a good stool softener.

—Rivers Cuomo

I need a facial!!

—Margaret Cho

Not that kind!

—Margaret Cho

Actually…

—Margaret Cho

I want both kinds

—Margaret Cho

Giving my self a soft tissue breast massage.
Ladies we have to keep those implants soft.

—*Heidi Montag*

I mean this in the best way, as a great
compliment 2 my wife & othr women I'm
sure. I luv menopause! The boobs r back
in town!

—*Eric Roberts*

Gonna take a late night steam shower……
Shave myself perfectly bald and crawl into
my huge bed!

—*Jenna Jameson*

Mid-orgasm, I had a vision: rows of evenly-
spaced plastic JFK halloween masks. Brains
are weirdos.

—*Sarah Silverman*

On my way for my yearly physical and anticipating that finger in my ass. Doesn't get better than this.

—*Howard Stern*

Not being weird but I'm walking Minnie and she has a cute butt. Not in a sexy way but in a Yoda rooting thru Luke's stuff way. Wiggly. Help.

—*Simon Pegg*

We Need next size up from super plus (tampons). what makes them think that little Q-tip will stop anything after a lifetime of penises?

—*Jenny McCarthy*

#KanyeWest

Love him or hate him, Kanye West certainly doesn't mind putting himself out there, whether he's talking about Satanism, complaining about airports, or giving his opinion on lipstick colors. Though he apologized (via Twitter) to Taylor Swift for famously stealing the microphone during the VMAs, people apparently didn't appreciate it when he joked about it.

Yo Britney, I'm really happy for you and I'mma let you be #1, but me and Jay-Z single is one of the best songs of all time! LOL

—*Kanye West*

I thought LOL signified a joke…. I didn't get the 2011 LOL doesn't signify a joke anymore memo…. LOL or something else I guess

—*Kanye West*

I swear my love bracelet and gold & diamond teeth always set off the metal detector

—*Kanye West*

Then I have to get "wonded" in front of everyone

—*Kanye West*

Greeeeeat : (......I feel sooooo much safer about the flight now that I've been disgraced in a public place lol

—*Kanye West*

I hate when I'm on a flight and I wake up with a water bottle next to me like oh great now I gotta be responsible for this water bottle

—*Kanye West*

It's like someone leaving a child at your door.... you gotta make sure it stays put.... you gotta hold it when the plane is landing....

—*Kanye West*

Is it super lonely and miserable to buy yourself a Cartier love bracelet....well I guess I do love my self lol!!!

—*Kanye West*

Tell everyone at the label only use Gothic or Helvetic fonts for email blast unless I otherwise approve

—*Kanye West*

Sometimes I get emotional over fonts

—*Kanye West*

I will be a better man, friend, role model, citizen, blogger, tweeter, artist, creator, giver, thinker, motivator and person. IFEELTHEGLOW

—*Kanye West*

@kanyewest sounds like somebody's pregnant!

—*Jimmy Kimmel*

hahahahahahahahahahahahhahahahahah
ahahahahahahahahahhahahahahahahaha
hahahhahahahahahahahahhahahahahaha
hahahahahhahahahahahahahahah aaand
140

—Kanye West

In response to the reaction of my album cover... "I'm deeply sorry if I haven't offended everybody"

—Kanye West

Please don't let girls start wearing dark lipstick again. I just think girls need to know that guys don't really like black lipstick

—Kanye West

She say.... well my hairdresser like it.... well tell me what your lipdresser says

—Kanye West

In the studio with Jay and B. Beyonce just explained to me that lip dressers are better known as make up artist lol

—*Kanye West*

I've got question about "the illuminati".... what is it exactly???.... and why do people think pop stars have a membership???!!! LOL

—*Kanye West*

Is illuminati and devil worshipping like the same thing.... do they have a social network that celebs can sign up for?

—*Kanye West*

What's better for devil worshipping Iphone or the Droid.... Does lucifer return text.... is he or she on Skype? Don't wanna be sexist

—*Kanye West*

Wasn't the world the world suppose to end "in the year 2000" (Conan voice)

—*Kanye West*

hoooold up…. last question…. does the devil wear Praaadaaaaaaaaa????!!!!

—*Kanye West*

an abortion can cost a ballin' nigga up to 50gs maybe a 100. Gold diggin' bitches be getting pregnant on purpose. **#STRAPUP** my niggas!

—*Kanye West*

It ain't happen to me but I know people.

—*Kanye West*

Yoko Says:

Dangle empty cans and bottles all over your body. Dance without making a sound.

—*Yoko Ono*

#CelebrityQuestionTime

It's not just Tyra and Larry King who love to ask questions on Twitter—lots of celebrities seek answers from their followers for all of life's questions.

Can I drink while I'm watching Barney?
—*Cindy Crawford*

What do you want for christmas????
—*Diddy*

Is jerry springer real?
—*Stephanie Pratt*

Does anyone know the right way to dig a poop hole in the mountains?
—*Jessica Simpson*

How come Dr's never get sick when they see sick people every day!

—*Kim Kardashian*

Why do we like asses?

—*Rivers Cuomo*

Ok there's a debate going. This is very important. In xo which is the hug? Which is the kiss?

—*Sara Gilbert*

Is barking up the wrong tree really that much worse than barking up the correct tree? They both seem like a huge waste of time to me.

—*Al Yankovic*

How many people hate the feeling of burping and nothing happens?

—*Ashley Olsen*

Did my asst Tiberious go home with snooki tonight???

—*Billy Bush*

Battle of the Sexes Question. Women how do u feel about Men who keep their socks on during sex? Does it ruin the mood or do u even care?

—*Ludacris*

#BOSQ: Women: what's ur favorite position U r having sex w/ ur man or when ur having sex w/ ur jump off? Is there a difference?

—*Ludacris*

Battle of the Sexes Question of the day. Is it anyway possible to turn a Ho into a Housewife? Explain.

—*Ludacris*

If you were a TV news reporter, would you feel sad having to talk about Justin Bieber's haircut?

—*R.L. Stine*

I'm thinking about getting a pet pig. Does this mean I'll have to give up pork?

—*Jessica Simpson*

why do people do crystal meth? why do people co-sign for cars?

—*Mary Carey*

Why did that soothsayer tell Caesar to "Beware the Ides of March" when he could've more helpfully said, "Beware the knives of stabbers"?

—*Conan O'Brien*

Is 630am too early for Nachos?

—*Lisa Rinna*

IS LIVING A LIE EASIER THAN FACING THE TRUTH? OR DO WE LIVE THE LIE IN HOPES OF CHANGING THE TRUTH?? im just asking?

—*Nelly*

do you know what's going on right now with Health Care? because I'm not sure I'm very clear? please tell me what you know… confusing?

—*Spencer Pratt*

Can someone find all the "Ethan & Theresa" montages from PASSIONS?

—*Eric Roberts*

Anybody here ever assigned to bang erasers together and get rid of the chalk dust?

—*Roger Ebert*

Do ants have dicks?

—*Kourtney Kardashian*

what isn't happening?

—*Zooey Deschanel*

Does anyone know the difference in the time, say if I were in like New York?

—*Serena Williams*

Yoko Says:

Is anything lopsided in your room? Would you like more lopsided things in your room?

—*Yoko Ono*

#JimGaffigan

Jim Gaffigan is a stand-up comedian and actor best known for jokes about Hot Pockets, his role on *My Boys*, and well…for tweeting funny things.

It's so embarrassing when I wrongly guess a kid's gender. Me "How old is he?" Parent "SHE is 23." Me "Wow, lot of hair"

—*Jim Gaffigan*

I don't care how many followers I lose chocolate covered strawberries suck. **#HeDidn't**

—*Jim Gaffigan*

"Oh here is a gigantic deformed tasteless strawberry let's cover it cheap-ass plastic chocolate" — Lame chef

—*Jim Gaffigan*

"Instead of waterboarding al-Qaeda prisoners why don't we just feed them chocolate covered strawberries."
— Torture expert

—*Jim Gaffigan*

Funny how "Congrats" always sounds like "You're crazy" after you tell someone you are about to have your 4th child.

—*Jim Gaffigan*

Just explained to my 3 kids that the new baby will not mean I love them any less, but I will have to let one of them go.

—*Jim Gaffigan*

If my wife makes one more crack about me eating all the baby food, I'm so out of here. **#IPaid4it**

—*Jim Gaffigan*

Why is it ok for people to touch my wife's pregnant belly but if I rub my gut on one stranger everyone wants me thrown out Dave & Busters?

—*Jim Gaffigan*

Hey 2-year-old girls, you look stupid trying to walk up stairs in a long dress. Figure it out.

—*Jim Gaffigan*

Have you ever been really full? What's that like?

—*Jim Gaffigan*

Overheard in my head: "The only thing crazier than a woman is a pregnant woman" **#tryingtolosefollowers?**

—*Jim Gaffigan*

"Pregnant women = crazy" is NOT something I SAID. It was something I THOUGHT and then shared with 500,000 strangers on the internet.

—*Jim Gaffigan*

I have more pictures of my kids than my Dad even looked at me.

—*Jim Gaffigan*

I hope one of the "7 Habits of Highly Successful People" is buying the book and not reading it.

—*Jim Gaffigan*

#Romance

There's nothing like a celebrity's idea of romance. Whether it is a grooming tip from New Kid on the Block Danny Wood or an appeal from rapper Juicy J, love is in the air.

Manscaping is standard.

—*Danny Wood*

Love tip. if your man isn't manscaping go out and by him a set of clippers with a note saying "t-bagging included".

—*Danny Wood*

Love tip…………Spice up your life orally!!!!!

—*Danny Wood*

I need a girl friend who's available? i will take u shoppin, pay 4 a boob job, tummy tuck, rent due, car loan, any bill I gotcha! lol

—*Juicy J*

I bet I'd be good at the sex.

—*Rob Delaney*

Lance Armstrong says the right response to high gas prices is to ride your bike. I say stay home and ride your partner!

—*Dr. Ruth*

Sometimes I fuk with my Timbs on

—*Kanye West*

Listening to a song called "Bitch Ass Trick". Needless to say… it's a love story.

—*Alyssa Milano*

Tip of the Day: Guys, a little dash of Baby Powder on the undercarriage keeps things fresh. You're welcome, ladies.

—*Dave Navarro*

If guys could get pregnant, you know you'd never hear them complaining about using condoms.

—Dr. Ruth

Who's a girl gotta blow to get some oral herpes in this town??

—Sarah Silverman

Of course "fanny smashing" is different pass time in the UK than it is in the US. Both have their merits though. Consent essential.

—Simon Pegg

I hate when people ask me how many calories are burned during sex. If that's a reason for having sex, then you're missing out big time.

—Dr. Ruth

Just passed a place advertising "Chocolate and Fruit-Flavored Brazilian Wax." I'm pretty sure my vagina lacks tastebuds.

—*Diablo Cody*

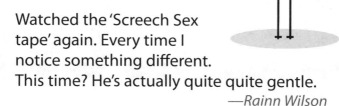

www.dicktowel.com crashed cause of too many hits. We will get it up ASAP! Don't want to keep you from your towels.

—*Charlie Day*

Watched the 'Screech Sex tape' again. Every time I notice something different. This time? He's actually quite quite gentle.

—*Rainn Wilson*

OMG hotness i wanna bang u

—*Soulja Boy*

Okay... That was a bit naughty... But you know what...? This Friday is just gonna be like that! The BACK RUB tonight? Naughty & Special!

—*Donnie Wahlberg*

Hornover: (Definition) what one wakes up with the morning after a night of getting too horny without release

—*Bow Wow*

Love to play R KELLY when writing a sex scene!!

—*Jackie Colllins*

Can i kiss u?

—*Chris Brown*

#idontunderstandwhy men like to have their nuts tickled

—*Khloe Kardashian*

Yoko Says:

Imagine painting all the statues in the world in the color of the sky.

—Yoko Ono

#Don'tCallJimCarreyCrazy

Please don't call Jim Carrey crazy. It hurts his feelings, and more importantly, he'll feel the need to prove you right.

The truth is I'm an intuitive, creative, and spiritual person. I'm healthier, smarter, and YES much more sane than u who say I'm crazy. cont-->

—Jim Carrey

I'm so sane in fact, that I have managed to transcend the pettiness of your kind my whole life! U suppressive types who r so afraid…cont-->

—Jim Carrey

that some1 might create something with lasting impact in this world, something u cannot find the faith or the courage to dream of…cont-->

—Jim Carrey

…the narrow vision of a CYCLOPS can perceive no depth. If any1 wants to cover one eye they can view the world as the CYCLOPS do…cont-->

—Jim Carrey

The vision of these narrow minds is flat, 2D, and those of us who see are something 2 fear. So I say to you who need 2 call me nuts…cont-->

—Jim Carrey

…#BOING Mother F%*kers #BOING Mother F%*kers #BOING!!! #BOING#BOING#BOING#BOING#BOING#BOING#BOING#BOING#BOING#BOING#BOING#BOING!!! {B^P

—Jim Carrey

#DannyDeVito

Danny DeVito's tweets are often nonsensical. But he's Danny Freaking DeVito! It's allowed.

Jiggle Balls Jiggle Balls.... oil them with myrrh.... O what fun it is for those balls when your the jiggel-er....

—*Danny DeVito*

Holy Shitballs! It's August 2nd!

—*Danny DeVito*

Great movie. IMAX in Burbank. Smaller screen but great picture. Like to bang one of those ten foot broads!

—*Danny DeVito*

NJ medherb! Troll foot need Ganga, Boo, Weed, Skunk, Pot, Sensa Milla Cush, Cronic, Trainwreck, Purple Cush, Orange Cush, Buda's earwax...

—*Danny DeVito*

CHARLIE DEE MAC DENNIS FRANK PETER LOIS MEG STEWIE CHRIS BRIAN GLEN TROLL FOOT HAITIANS FOOD KIDS SHELTER CLOTHING WATER DOCTORS SPIRIT LIFE

—Danny DeVito

Mykonos just came onfilling the house with the fleet foxes I dig this bunch of talented MoFo's hope the day is infused with their harmony

—Danny DeVito

Anyone want to roast a pig and get a good Mai Tai drunk going

—Danny DeVito

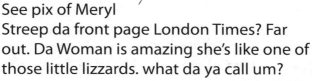

See pix of Meryl Streep da front page London Times? Far out. Da Woman is amazing she's like one of those little lizzards. what da ya call um?

—Danny DeVito

#Gross

Celebrities can be seriously disgusting. None more so than Ke$ha, who is ACTUALLY COLLECTING HUMAN TEETH.

I've received 1 tooth from a fan. I made it into a necklace. But now I really wanna make a fan tooth necklace to wear to an awards show.

—*Ke$ha*

i recycle bodyparts. im looking at all my crazybeautiful fans teeth right now!! i got a box of em and ive never been so excited !!!

—*Ke$ha*

Peanut butter & jelly tacos

—*Soulja Boy*

LOL! hell the fuck naw i aint eating that shit. somebody just hit me on aim and said they making some i was like WTF i gotta tweet that LOL

—*Soulja Boy*

so I just put this zit cream on my face that has sulfur in it and now my face smells like an egg fart. its making me SICK!

—*Kelly Osbourne*

Happy Valentines Day!!!! Its too bad "Eat out my butt," doesn't fit on one of those little candy hearts.

—*Chris Pratt*

I hope the inventor of the Egg McMuffin won the Nobel Prize in Fart Odor Replication.

—*Rob Delaney*

love reading your responses to my corns! **#IGotCornsOnMyToesCuz** I've been wearing heels 4 so long. got to be comfy sometimes though.

—*Tyra Banks*

Not complainin' but everytime I lifted my arms, I was like "damn who stinks like that!" Then I realized I was the only one in the room!

—Sherri Shepherd

Oh man, I just stepped on a snail. I wouldn't mind but it really crunched. Muthafucka might as well have screamed. Will feel bad for 8 mins.

—Simon Pegg

my puppy's paws smell like fritto's!

—Stephanie Pratt

If I paid you $500, would you taste my puke?

—Andrew WK

This is great! A lot of people are into my offer! I'm organizing this. $500 per person, for tasting ¼ cup of my puke. More soon…

—Andrew WK

I just got the perfect clothes for the sexiest rapper alive. Ladies u must see my outfits! I'm cleaner than catfish pussy.

—Soulja Boy

Omg my boyfriend made me a pickle pancake…yeahhhh he's amazing!

—Snooki

Get real everybody, if you love pickles like I do, pickles are good with anything. Let me liveeeE! :)

—Snooki

The dude next to me was picking his nose. I'm serious!!! Like he was fingerfucking his nostril!!!!

—Margaret Cho

I'm sure I just pissed off a bunch of people who disagree with me…but it's better to be pissed OFF…than pissed ON.

—Star Jones

A man in a 3 piece suit just yelled "She hasn't been laid in so long, she pussy farts mummy dust!" **#ILoveNewYorkCity**

—*Nicole Richie*

Last night's reference to "come ice cream" should have read "some ice cream." It's called a Freudian slip. Sorry about that.

—*Hugh Hefner*

…that had nothing to do with him finding a condom in his soup—right?

—*R.L. Stine*

Yoko Says:

Tape the sound of the moon fading at dawn. Give it to your mother to listen to when she's in sorrow.

—*Yoko Ono*

#RogerEbert

Roger Ebert once wrote that Twitter represented the end of civilization, but after losing his lower jaw to cancer he came to rely on—and love—using the site. In fact, a play was created based on his tweets.

Self-help books are bullshit. Read a good book. That'll help you.

—*Roger Ebert*

Mullets decreed illegal in Iran. At last, something we agree on.

—*Roger Ebert*

In the past, spell-checker has changed "preacher" to "pirate" and "wholesome" to "whoreson." It thinks my name is Robert.

—*Roger Ebert*

I wish people would stop calling me "Mr. Ebert." That's as bad as "young man." I'm old, and I'm Roger.

—*Roger Ebert*

Advised I should stick to tweeting on topics I know something about. Then attacked for tweeting about Japanese breast pillows.

—*Roger Ebert*

Donald Trump's hair affects me like one of those optical illusions where you can't tell whether the steps are going up or going down.

—*Roger Ebert*

Cleavage. It speaks to us from the time before memory of love, comfort, warmth, softness and food. Cleavage. Oh yes. Cleavage.

—*Roger Ebert*

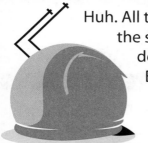

Huh. All these years and never the slightest twinge of a desire to take a Polar Bear Plunge.

—*Roger Ebert*

Have any children been named "Google?"

—*Roger Ebert*

#Huh?

Sometimes celebrity tweets are a little odd.

Watch very closely as the magical angel and I are swallowed by the rainbow twister, and left stranded on the Glitter Way.

—*Lady Gaga*

Showertime over&out. catch u on da up side tell yor story walking go see if it's rainin round da corner send dat guy ot fo a bucket of steam

—*Danny DeVito*

When very young I thought Mrs Lincoln and my mother were in hospital together, giving birth to Abe and me.

—*Judy Blume*

Lying hear reading scripts...., purple haze all in my brain....thinking of stuff.... usually pretty perceptive but my radar feels occluded...

—*Kirstie Alley*

Don't look in your rear view mirror unless you're prepared to facilitate the inevitable.

—*Gary Busey*

And now I go to work with blood in 1 eye and a tear in the other, ill hunt you down and call you Brother!!

—*Dog the Bounty Hunter*

Europeans have a better understanding that animals r people n fur coats. Euros r oft seen n fine restaurants with their humans.

—*Shirley MacLaine*

Preemptive justification supposes astute classification.

—*Gary Busey*

television is weirdos judging weirdos viewed by weirdos who are just glad there are weirder weirdos out there. like me DAMN IT! %^(

—*Jim Carrey*

History=pop culture

—*Leighton Meester*

Sometimes I forget to breathe!

—*Spencer Pratt*

#youwishyouweremybutt

—*T-Pain*

The more you stare at your thumbs, the weirder they look.

—*Kristen Bell*

HEY EVERYONE I'M LAUGHING!

—*Boy George*

what am i a bowl of fruit that peels itself? im nota thing to be consumed.…

—*John Cusack*

My 5000th follower will be sealed in an interdimensional hourglass at the edge of the universe. Not ligerally, of course.

—*Gary Busey*

Fuck A Mixtape!

—*T.I.*

"Damn right I just quoted myself"
~ Nick Cannon

—Nick Cannon

I wish my ears were cameras.

—Gary Busey

Yoko Says:

Grapefruit is a hybrid of lemon and orange. Snow is a hybrid of wish and lament.

—Yoko Ono

#ScottBaio

Scott Baio seems very angry at the world. What's the matter, Chachi?

When I was young & watched Award shows, people would really sing. Not lip-synch & act like an idiot. That Ga Ga girl is Gag Gag.

—*Scott Baio*

Yes, I can have an opinion because 100 years ago I had 2 LP's. I HAD TO SING LIVE EVERY TIME. (I can't sing 4 shit but the $ was good)

—*Scott Baio*

Today the world "Celebrity" doesn't always mean "Actor". I'd like to think of myself as an "Actor" **@teddykay**

—*Scott Baio*

177

Funny thing is I've jumped to almost 5000 because ppl like to hate. You'd think they wouldn't follow. I block'em & play golf.

—*Scott Baio*

If I'm racist, don't think I would have Directed shows like The Parkers & The Wayans Bros. or worked 41 eps w/ Victoria Rowell on D. Murder

—*Scott Baio*

#ConanO'Brien

Conan O'Brien joined Twitter after his controversial departure from NBC. Though obviously no longer unemployed, the famous redhead still tweets for his millions of followers.

Today I connected all the freckles on my arm with a Sharpie. It spells out RIKSAZ9LIRK. Clearly I am THE Chosen One.
—*Conan O'Brien*

Product placement is so pervasive these days it makes me want to Doritos.
—*Conan O'Brien*

I came in second to Lady Gaga in the Artist's category of the Time 100. Once again, I'm penalized for not wearing a bra that shoots fire.
—*Conan O'Brien*

Thinking of removing my calf implants. My eyes are up here, ladies.

—*Conan O'Brien*

@ConanOBrien when I applied for Adonis DNA, 6'8", red hair, freckles & genius was taken. My shot at late night…over, crack here I come! c

—*Charlie Sheen*

Thanks **@charliesheen** for the compliment. To clarify, I'm 7'1", a super genius, and those aren't freckles – it's male menopausal acne.

—*Conan O'Brien*

I prefer to have my affairs over Twitter because I usually can't last more than 140 characters.

—*Conan O'Brien*

From the outside, some Korean funeral homes look just like Korean massage parlors. My sincerest apologies to the entire Myong family.

—*Conan O'Brien*

Had that dream again last night where the GEICO lizard makes me hold his legs down while he does sit-ups.

—*Conan O'Brien*

Yoko Says:

Whisper your dream to a cloud. Ask the cloud to remember it.

—*Yoko Ono*

#CourtneyLove

Courtney Love's Twitter rants were so over-the-top, she was slapped with several libel suits in response to her tweets. In fact, she was forced to pay a fashion designer $430,000 after accusing her of being a drug dealer and embezzler on Twitter. Here, she feuds with singer Lily Allen, though one would think they could bond over their mutual distaste for punctuation and capital letters.

just clearing a couple of things up. Courtney Love and I did NOT have a bust up at the NME's. There was an exchange of words, yes

—Lily Allen

she's upset because she ahs got it into her head that i put a lock on some dresses for the brit awards. she's made no secret of this and,

—Lily Allen

when i saw her at the NME'S she tried to talk to me and i told her to shut up stop spreading stupid rumours about me.

—Lily Allen

[posts picture of Courtney Love] sorry, that was mean. enuff of these juvenile musings, i should never have risen to the bait. Silly lily.

—*Lily Allen*

oh **@lilyroseallen** tweeted that pic? thats just baby brat nonsense we are NOT having a "FUED" WOULDNT DEIGN TO post a pic of her thights.

—*Courtney Love*

@lilyroseallen the night you home invaded me did all the blow ive ever seen in my home wouldnt leave and blamed ME for yr shit show? thighs?

—*Courtney Love*

Oh shit…did i just SHOUT at CARNEGIE HALL? i am NOT making excuses. well i am, perhaps it was the curse of the kook. hangs head.

—*Courtney Love*

running a bath cos I have to wash my **#BigFuckingHair** and possibly just possibly **#TheJoshuaTreeOfVaginas** who knows who am i to say?

—*Courtney Love*

men are beyond confusing

—*Courtney Love*

every blue moon i take an ambien, last night i did, its vile, i texted three people utter gibberish, and woke up spaced out as hell. No!

—*Courtney Love*

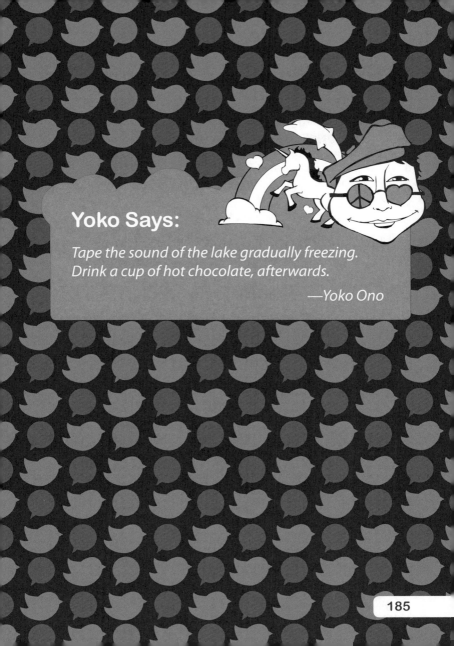

Yoko Says:

Tape the sound of the lake gradually freezing.
Drink a cup of hot chocolate, afterwards.

—Yoko Ono

#Snooze

There are the drama queens and the drunks, the comedians and the name-droppers—but the most offensive of all celebrity tweets is the boring one. Listen celebrities, we're not following you to hear about what you ate for dinner or if you like turtles—that's why we have Facebook friends we ignore.

I am addicted to Italian & Chinese food.
—*Jackie Collins*

At some point I transtioned from despising string beans and snap peas to seeking them out constantly. I just realized this today.
—*Ben Stiller*

I love pencils.
—*Erykah Badu*

My dog Poker is very reasonable. I like that.
—*Neil Diamond*

Why are women's shower products so much nicer than men's? Most men's shower products feel like sandpaper
—*Ryan Seacrest*

Pilates has saved me
—*Alec Baldwin*

Hey everyone, I've been taking a short twitter break. I couldn't think of anything interesting to say but now I can
—*Venus Williams*

I want to download this movie Night at the Roxbury but they don't have it on itunes. Dang they don't have Footloose either, lol
—*Venus Williams*

Ah twitter you're my go to guy when I have nothing important to say.

—Pete Wentz

Turtles are amazing. Really.

—Ben Stiller

I'm not so sure about green gummi bears… they taste funny

—Holly Madison

Blah dum Dee oh blah dum doo blah dum dob, oh blah doom Dee blah doom doo blah dum Dee blah dum doo, I have a blue house with a blue window

—Benjamin Madden

its 12:34!! anytime its 12:34 or 11:11 i make a wish!!

—Audrina Partridge

Mirrors are awesome!!!!!!!

—*Danny Wood*

I love rice cripsies!!!!

—*Diddy*

I love homemade turkey sandwiches

—*Kristin Cavallari*

Drinking New York city tap water

—*Kanye West*

I had a nightmare that I slept without my nose tape on thank God it wasn't true!

—*Heidi Montag*

i should be married

—*Amanda Bynes*

When I'm a house wife my husband can call me kitty or better yet wifey!

—*Amanda Bynes*

i like wearing light pink or peach lipstick/gloss. Why do sum girls wear black/dark purple lipstick? in movie i would but in real life? no

—*Amanda Bynes*

I gotta say.…I'm mildly obsessed and madly in love with.… My glue gun.

—*Tori Spelling*

Yesterday was fun! I love the color pink :)-

—*Paris Hilton*

Only 15 days til Christmas!!!! "I can't even know what to say!!!" :)

—*Mariah Carey*

Yesterday was Thursday…

—*Nicole Richie*

I hate vegetables.

—*Kristin Chenoweth*

#GotJokes?

There are all sorts of celebrities cracking jokes on Twitter, though some are more successful than others.

It's a good thing I was born a girl, otherwise I'd be a drag queen

—*Dolly Parton*

I look just like the girls next door.… if you happen to live next door to an amusement park.

—*Dolly Parton*

TO ALL L.A. PRIVATE SCHOOL KIDS. as someone who was forced to endure the idiocy of your world here is my message 2u: **#youcantdj**. stop trying

—*Frances Bean Cobain*

I got my cat a passport- he got arrested for carrying cat-nip, which is cute. And a gun which is less so.

—Russell Brand

How long after Grandma was run over by a reindeer did they write that song, because they seem awfully cavalier about this brutal attack.

—Paul Scheer

Don't let the sun go down on you, because it will burn your dick off.

—Jimmy Kimmel

Something very sad about the fact I haven't read Moby Dick, but I have read the Kindergarten Cop Wikipedia page.

—Aziz Ansari

Just got a creepy "God wanted me to tell you" message on MySpace. You'd think God would have moved on to Facebook by now.

—*Dave Navarro*

I decided to get Married today!!! I feel like a new man! Wedding is planned for valentines day!!! Your all welcome!! Feb 14th. Let's go!

—*Diddy*

I also became vegan today!!!! :)

—*Diddy*

Weddings off. She aint sign the prenup!!! Lol. I'm just bullsitin. Sorry I'm bored today! And I'm not a vegan. Let's goooo!

—*Diddy*

I like to smile at strangers. Sometimes they smile back. And every once in a while a person gets really creeped out and it's all worth it.

—*Chris Pratt*

Every time a sexy woman jumps out of a giant cake there is at least one guy who is bummed about the cake being ruined.

—*Jonah Hill*

I get no sponsorship from anything I tweet about. I don't need the cashola. I'm privately wealthy from trademarking "OMG".

—*Mindy Kaling*

Every time a celebrity posts an "inspirational" tweet, they should be forced to drink a pint of their signature perfume.

—*Rob Delaney*

Huh, what's this?…Iranair flight at the next gate. Ahhh…the warm, full body sensation of not-fucking-tempting-at-all.

—*Will Arnett*

I saw a woman with a huge chest tattoo that read "Only God Can Judge Me". Cool, but I've already gone ahead & done some prelim work.

—*Joel McHale*

When Im 60 I want to look like Meryl Streep. And I mean EXACTLY like Meryl Streep.

—*Rainn Wilson*

#AdrianneCurry

Adrianne Curry rose to pseudo-fame by winning the first season of *America's Next Top Model*. Then she moved on to *The Surreal Life*, dating Peter Brady (Christopher Knight), and getting her own reality show, *My Fair Brady*. When she's not tweeting about how much she dislikes Tyra Banks, she's whining about the hassle of being thin and naming her privates.

Biography called wanting2interview me for Tyra Banks story. Naturally, I declined. She wouldnt want me on it, she nixes my image from ANTM

—*Adrianne Curry*

One last thing, tyra did NOT want me2go on surreal life&tried2stop me. she thought it would ruin her shows image. She has been quoted sayin so

—*Adrianne Curry*

This broad let her dog shit in my yard&then jumped her car2leave&said she'd clean it later. So,I spit on her car&told her I'll clean it later

—*Adrianne Curry*

going to pump some iron! Society looks at physically fit women like myself and say we r 2 skinny. I say, YOU are too FAT! go2thegym!

—*Adrianne Curry*

yay! im a level 16 on WoW now!

—*Adrianne Curry*

It's official. 2day I have been married2my husband longer than his last2marriages…I beat them bitches out…&it looks like i'll keep going! ;)

—*Adrianne Curry*

whooo! just got done working out.…i return to world of warcraft mon night! have only played once since chris&I announced our split :(

—*Adrianne Curry*

concerning my personal life, i think people need to mind their own business&fix their own failing lives b4 judging mine. hahaha

—*Adrianne Curry*

Decided2rename my vagina from"Ralph"2"Bandersnatch". Though Ralph was funny, I believe my womanhood identifies w/the bandersnatch more ;)

—*Adrianne Curry*

FYI, I got my tits done cause I had a A&C cup! If men had1ball that hung2their knee&the other was nicely tucked under, they would fix it2 ;)

—*Adrianne Curry*

I always laugh, people jump on me to tell me I'm not famous…like I dont know my own pecking order. Bottom of the barrel, baby ;)

—*Adrianne Curry*

#JustWrong

Whether it's the subject matter or the location (a funeral, really?), there are some celebrity tweets that seem even more inappropriate than usual.

Alabama is so hot it must've been a relief for the civil rights protesters when the fire hoses were turned on them.
—*Michael Ian Black*

Ratio of people offended vs. people who found my last tweet funny: 12:1.
—*Michael Ian Black*

This may be my last tweet. Anne Geddes has surrounded my home & is demanding to photograph my baby. I will kill him first.
—*Rob Delaney*

N the car headed 2 the funeral!
—*NeNe Leakes*

If your kid starts playing peek-a-boo with me at a restaurant, I'll flirt right back…and I'm GOOD at it. **#thingsiwishididntoverhearatchilis**

—*Jonah Hill*

I want to blow your mind cuz I don't (necessarily) have to cup you balls in the process.

—*Carrie Fisher*

I kno he peed in a lil' girl eye, but R. Kelly's new song "when a woman loves" is beautiful.

—*Marlon Wayans*

People never believe me when I tell them my Kindergarten teacher's name was Bumblebee Dickfiddler.

—*Rob Delaney*

Tweeting from the White House bathroom!

—*John Legend*

Who would have ever thought that my tits would help raise $44,500.00+ for charity?? WOW IM STUNNED! LOVE U!

—*Tila Tequila*

In other news, Jay Leno caught fucking the tailpipe of an outrageous antique car.

—*Diablo Cody*

Yoko Says:

Sit at the dock. Watch the seagulls dance. Dance with them in your mind. Keep dancing until you feel you can hear their heartbeats.

—*Yoko Ono*

#BieberMania

After Justin Bieber was vaulted into the spotlight, he soon became an American obsession—not just for teen girls, but for celebrities as well, apparently.

Barbara walters just came backstage earlier. I hit on her… Just joking around though. Think she liked it Haha

—*Justin Bieber*

they are not allowing me to come into the mall. if you dont leave I and my fans will be arrested as the police just told us.

—*Justin Bieber*

Feels good to be a kid

—*Justin Bieber*

girls of london...please dont bang on the windows of the car when we're moving. u can get hurt. no need for that. i got love for all of u :)

—*Justin Bieber*

so alot of u r tweeting me wanting to know if i died again. turns out im ok. had to check...but im still living. wasnt sure.... but....im ok :)

—*Justin Bieber*

cant really talk but just did a press conference with the big fella **@the_real_shaq** . Shaq held it down and did the talking 4 me.

—*Justin Bieber*

i got ur back big bieber RT **@justinbieber** just did press conference w/ big fella @**the_real_shaq**. Shaq held it down & did the talking 4 me

—*Shaquille O'Neal*

@**justinbieber** is tweeting about me again. He's obsessed! Which new song is about me, beebz? If it's "Eenie Meenie", we have a problem.

—*Conan O'Brien*

It's my birthday tomorrow! All I want for my birthday is world peace, and a lock of @**JustinBieber**'s hair.

—*Ellen DeGeneres*

Met Justin Bieber tonight on Letterman. Told him to hang in there, things will happen for him ventually.

—*Ben Stiller*

#DrugsAreBad

Those were celebrity tweets. These are celebrity tweets on drugs. Any questions?

Today is National Marijuana Day. A day when…uh…wow, Wolf Blitzer is SO funny.
—*Steve Martin*

Can u believe, I can handle a drug-free water birth at home no prob, yet, I'm a complete wuss when it comes to dental work. Go figure.
—*Ricki Lake*

Druuuuuggssss are kiccckkkking iiiinnnnnnn.
—*Ricki Lake*

Pot&exercise = great idea. I sat &read People on the bike for 16 mins b4 noticing I hadn't started peddling
—*Sarah Silverman*

SMOKE WEED EVERYDAY especially on **#puffpuffpasstuesdays**

—*Snoop Dogg*

excuse me, people? It's nice and all your sending me these "bong hits", but I do NOT smoke schwag and havent since I was 13, so no thanks ;)

—*Adrianne Curry*

Some fancy entertainment people are smoking crack on the balcony next to mine. And I'm playing scrabble. I feel very uncool. Sane but uncool

—*Moby*

Its 4/20. Happy birthday weed.

—*Bob Saget*

Congratulations to all my fellow non-Emmy nominees. We're the real winners… we get to watch the show stoned and in our underwear.

—*George Lopez*

Bout to go up to VH1… They are doing a show on the CRACK era and they called me as a expert. Ain't that a bitch. Haha.

—*Ice-T*

Sorry I am quiet today. I am celebrating 4/20 by getting high with my children.

—*Michael Ian Black*

"Meth is nature's pancakes.…"
— A breakfast tip from the Meth Council.

—*Patton Oswalt*

Seriously, busting 77 Willie Nelson for pot possesion on his tour bus?? He should get a medal for having a tour bus at 77.

—*Ben Stiller*

btw, I'm not high.

—*Will Arnett*

If Miley Cyrus had just hit that bong dressed as Hannah Montana, no one would've known it was her.

—*Seth McFarlane*

Sorry guys. I had no idea. Just saw this stuff for the first time myself. Im so sad. There is much beyond my control right now.

—*Billy Ray Cyrus*

Wait Miley got high? Where have I been?! Buried under the tinsel obiv. **@mileycyrus** meet my friend **@snoopdoog**.… He'll hook ya up!

—*Katy Perry*

Yoko Says:

Carry a heavy object on your back. Dance as swiftly as you can.

—Yoko Ono

#RealHousewivesOfClassCity

The Real Housewives franchise of shows has turned some already-rich women—and reunion host Andy Cohen—into overnight celebrities. *The Real Housewives* tweets are probably not too surprising. For example, Atlanta's NeNe Leakes and Kim Zolciak feud on Twitter, just like they do in real life.

@bravoandy watched the entire atlanta marathon yesterday and I am converted. Nene leakes is the most charming thing since jean harlow.

—*Isaac Mizrahi*

Kick rocks trashy whore!

—*NeNe Leakes*

Guns loaded baby! U better bring yo best game! It's going down! I hope the transvestite can get yo back! Now what

—*NeNe Leakes*

God has a way of teaching people about the laws of Karma. Side note, I am extremely happy and will supersede, THX for all your support

—Kim Zolciak

Unreal how ppl spend there days obsessed with me, go around trying sabotage me It's a trip too bad my voice is bigger than yours will ever b

—Kim Zolciak

People are so obsessed, I wish they would get a life! Its so flattering people spend hours, days etc talking abt me. Cracks me up.

—Kim Zolciak

Look if you all want to tweet some crazy sh*t to me, I recommend you cut your head off and grow yourself a scab.

—Kim Zolciak

getting my mamogram

—Danielle Staub

the high low fight was infamous for it conveys that no one should have to put up with a bully. always stay up here with me with integrity.

—*Kelly Bensimon*

prepare yourself for my book The Naked Truth by Danielle Staub my life ~ my way!!

—*Danielle Staub*

Have you ever thanked a Bloody Mary before?

—*Kim Zolciak*

What should I change my license plate 2?? Give me some ideas…

—*Kim Zolciak*

@[**Bethenny Frankel**] you looked amazing last night. I am sorry if you think I over consumed you. All I did was try to be your friend.

—*Jill Zarin*

Today is the day I became an elephant. went to bed w a cute bump. woke up like a swollen beast. good news: the boobs aren't out of control.

—*Bethenny Frankel*

There should be a warning before Real Housewives eps that says UM, THIS IS NOT ACCEPTABLE BEHAVIOR

—*Sarah Silverman*

Yoko Says:

I know about saying goodbye. It's not easy, is it? But you should know that on a real level, There's No Goodbye!

—*Yoko Ono*

Don't forget
to party.
—*Andrew WK*

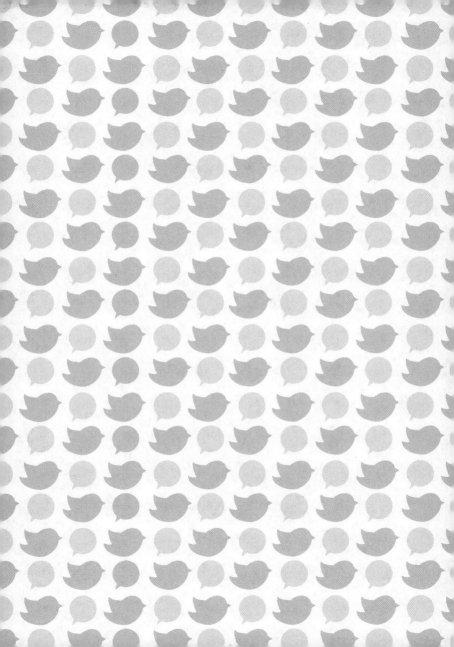